CAMBRIDGE LIBRARY C

Books of enduring scholarly

Linguistics

From the earliest surviving glossaries and translations to nineteenth century academic philology and the growth of linguistics during the twentieth century, language has been the subject both of scholarly investigation and of practical handbooks produced for the upwardly mobile, as well as for travellers, traders, soldiers, missionaries and explorers. This collection will reissue a wide range of texts pertaining to language, including the work of Latin grammarians, groundbreaking early publications in Indo-European studies, accounts of indigenous languages, many of them now extinct, and texts by pioneering figures such as Jacob Grimm, Wilhelm von Humboldt and Ferdinand de Saussure.

An Elementary Grammar with Full Syllabary and Progresssive Reading Book, of the Assyrian Language, in the Cuneiform Type

Archibald Henry Sayce (1845–1933) became interested in Middle Eastern languages and scripts while still a teenager. Old Persian and Akkadian cuneiform had recently been deciphered, and in the early 1870s the translation of part of the epic tale of Gilgamesh attracted considerable publicity. Based at Oxford, the young philologist Sayce published several books on Assyrian in quick succession. In the preface to this 1875 teaching grammar/reader, he notes that in just three years since the publication of his grammar for specialists (also reissued in this series), Assyrian had become a 'popular' subject, with students 'flocking in from all sides'. His book was written in response to the demand for beginners' books that were similar to those available for Greek or Hebrew. The texts that follow the syllabary and outline grammar are accompanied by transliterations and translations, with substantial accompanying notes on vocabulary, grammar points, and Hebrew cognates.

An Elementary Grammar

with Full Syllabary
and Progresssive Reading Book,

of

the Assyrian Language,

in the Cuneiform Type

Archibald Henry Sayce

CAMBRIDGE
UNIVERSITY PRESS

University Printing House, Cambridge, CB2 8BS, United Kingdom

Cambridge University Press is part of the University of Cambridge.
It furthers the University's mission by disseminating knowledge in the pursuit of
education, learning and research at the highest international levels of excellence.

www.cambridge.org
Information on this title: www.cambridge.org/9781108077958

© in this compilation Cambridge University Press 2014

This edition first published 1875
This digitally printed version 2014

ISBN 978-1-108-07795-8 Paperback

This book reproduces the text of the original edition. The content and language reflect
the beliefs, practices and terminology of their time, and have not been updated.

Cambridge University Press wishes to make clear that the book, unless originally published
by Cambridge, is not being republished by, in association or collaboration with,
or with the endorsement or approval of, the original publisher or its successors in title.

ARCHAIC CLASSICS.

ASSYRIAN GRAMMAR,

AND

READING BOOK.

ARCHAIC CLASSICS.

AN

ELEMENTARY GRAMMAR;

WITH

FULL SYLLABARY

AND PROGRESSIVE READING BOOK,

OF

THE ASSYRIAN LANGUAGE,

IN THE

CUNEIFORM TYPE.

BY

THE REV. A. H. SAYCE, M.A.

FELLOW AND TUTOR OF QUEEN'S COLLEGE, OXFORD.

Author of "An Assyrian Grammar;" and "The Principles of Comparative Philology.

Multæ terricolis linguæ, cœlestibus una.

LONDON:

SAMUEL BAGSTER AND SONS,

15, PATERNOSTER ROW.

TO

THE PRESIDENT AND MEMBERS

OF THE

SOCIETY OF BIBLICAL ARCHÆOLOGY

THIS VOLUME

IS

DEDICATED BY THE AUTHOR.

CONTENTS.

PREFACE.

THE following pages have been written in connection with my lectures upon Assyrian philology, which were commenced in the early part of 1875 under the auspices of the Society of Biblical Archæology, and through the exertions of Mr. W. R. Cooper, the Secretary of the Society. An endeavour has been made for the first time to smooth over the difficulties which beset the entrance to the study of the Assyrian inscriptions, and so attract students to this new and important branch of research. When my " Assyrian Grammar" was published, three years ago, a knowledge of the language was still confined to the few, and there seemed little prospect that the small band of Assyriologues would be much increased for a long while to come. My work was therefore addressed to two classes of readers; to those who were already able to read the inscriptions, and could appreciate a grammar which entered into details and points of scholarship, and to those who were acquainted with the better-known Semitic languages, but wished to learn something of the new dialect which had been so unexpectedly revealed, and promised to throw such a flood of light on Semitic philology in general. The prospect, however, that three years ago seemed so distant has been more than realised. Assyrian has become a "popular" subject; and the world of scholars which once looked with distrust upon the labours of the decipherers, has at last awakened to their interest and importance. Students are flocking in from all sides, and elementary grammars and progressive reading-books, like those which initiate the pupil into Hebrew or Greek, are needed and called for.

The present volume is intended to meet this demand. The cuneiform type which has been freely used throughout will accustom the eye of the reader to the forms of the characters, and as all transliterated words are divided into syllables, even where the Assyrian text is not added, he will be able to reduce them into their original forms. Care has been taken not to burden the memory with unnecessary matter; and practical experience has proved that tabular lists of nouns, verbs, and particles, such as are given in the second part of the book, are the best means for impressing the rudiments of a new language upon the mind. A separate chapter on the syntax has been omitted, since any attempt to enter into details would be inconsistent with the plan of the Grammar, while it has been found more convenient to state those few cases of importance in which Assyrian differs from the syntactical usage of other languages in those places of the accidence to which they naturally belong. The notes appended to each of the reading-lessons are designed to lead the student on to a more advanced and independent acquaintance with the language, and so complete the work of a practical and elementary grammar.

The main difficulty is the Syllabary, the larger part of which will sooner or later have to be learnt by heart. The beginner is advised first to commit to memory the characters which express open syllables, given in pp. 46 and 47, as well as the Determinative Prefixes and Affixes given in p. 48, and then to work at the *monosyllabic* closed syllables. Experience alone can show him what are the commoner and more favourite values with which a character is used; and he must be content to be continually a learner, keeping the Syllabary constantly at his side for purposes of reference, and remembering that any endeavour to learn the *whole* Syllabary is a needless and useless task. He will soon come to know what characters and what values are most frequently employed, and what ideographs are most likely to occur in the inscriptions.

The hieroglyphic origin of the Syllabary, and its adaptation to the wants of a foreign language, will give the key to many of the difficulties he will meet with. Its Accadian inventors spoke an agglutinative dialect; and each hieroglyphic, which in course of time came to be corrupted into a cuneiform character (like the modern Chinese), originally expressed the sound of the word denoting the object or idea for which it stood. The same picture could stand for more ideas than one, and might therefore be pronounced in more than one way, so that when the Semitic Assyrians (or rather Babylonians) borrowed the cuneiform system of writing, using what were words in Accadian as mere phonetic values, polyphony became inevitable, and the same character represented several phonetic powers. Even in Accadian the characters could be employed phonetically as well as ideographically; and the Assyrians, while turning the dictionary of the Accadians into a huge syllabary, did not forget the hieroglyphic origin of the writing, but reserved to themselves the power of using a character not only as the representative of a syllabic sound, but also as an ideograph to which of course a Semitic pronunciation was attached.

Many of the characters exhibit their primitive form at the first glance; ⌐ for instance, clearly standing for "the tongue of a balance." In other cases the resemblance to the objects originally signified is not very visible in the simplified forms of the characters as used in Assyria, and we have to go back to the archaic Babylonian type to detect the likeness. Thus ⊰⟊ has lost all resemblance to "the sun;" and it is not until we remember the archaic ⟡ that we discover the circle which stood for the great luminary of day. A large number of characters are compound, and when they are used ideographically their meaning can often be determined by considering what is the meaning of the separate characters of which they are made up. Thus ⟨cuneiform⟩ is "a mouth," and ⟨cuneiform⟩ "a drop of water;" the compound ⟨cuneiform⟩ therefore naturally denotes the act of "drinking." So, again, the Assyrian ⟨cuneiform⟩ "a month" is the simplified form of the archaic ⟨cuneiform⟩, where ⟨cuneiform⟩ the numeral 30 (expressing the 30 days of the month), is placed within the circle of the sun.

The use of polyphones no doubt increases the difficulty of decipherment, but the student will find that practically it is not so embarrassing as it would seem at first sight to be.   The Assyrians intended their inscriptions to be read (at all events except in the case of texts like those of the astrological tablets, which were addressed to the initiated only), and accordingly adopted all possible means of obviating the disadvantages of a polyphonic system of writing.   The following rules should be observed by the student in selecting one of the many values a given character may bear :—

(1) The existence of an ideograph should never be assumed, unless it is indicated by a phonetic complement, or unless the inscription (like the astrological ones generally) is written throughout ideographically rather than phonetically.

(2) Where two characters come together (such as *ca* and *ac*), the first of which ends with the same vowel as that with which the second begins, we may infer that they form one closed syllable (as *cac*).

(3) If a character expresses an open syllable (as *ri*) as well as a closed one (as *tal*), the open is to be preferred to the closed (unless contra-indicated).

(4) Those values are to be selected which offer a triliteral (or biliteral) root, and not a pluriliteral one.

(5) Notice must be taken of the final or initial consonant of the character which precedes or follows the one we are considering, as the Assyrians frequently doubled a consonant to show what value is to be chosen in a doubtful case. Thus ⬡𝍐 𝍐⬡ must be read *dan-nin*, as *dan* alone out of the many possible values of the first character ends with *n*.

(6) A character which denotes a syllable beginning with a vowel is very rarely used after one which ends with a consonant.

(7) Words and lines end together, and proper names, &c., are pointed out by Determinative Prefixes and Affixes.

(8) Variant readings and variant forms of the same root must be carefully observed, as they often decide the pronunciation of a word where all other means fail.

(9) Experience will show that common use had set apart one or two values of a given character which were preferably employed to all others.

(10) Those values must be adopted which bring out a correct grammatical form, or enable us to compare the Assyrian word (should the context determine its meaning) with a similar root in the cognate languages.

It is not so much the existence of polyphones, however, that forms the chief defect in the Assyrian mode of writing. The phonology of the inventors of the writing was not the same as the phonology of the Assyrians, and sounds which were distinct in Assyrian had to be represented by one and the same sign. ⬡𝍐 is both *hu* or *u* (הו and או and ו) and *yu* (יו), 𝍐 *za* and *tsa*, ⬡𝍐 *da* and *dha*, ⬡𝍐 *di* and *dhi*, ⬡𝍐 *e* (ע) and a modified ו, ⬡ *bu* and *pu*. Similarly the same characters denoted both *m* and *v*, and no distinction was made between final *d*, *dh*, and *t ;* *b* and *p ; g, c,* and *k :* and *z, s, ts,* and even *s ;* while closed syllables might begin as well as end with any of these doubtful letters. The uncertainty which results from this as to the initial or final letter of a syllable would naturally not press upon the Assyrian; but it is the main difficulty against which the modern decipherer has to contend, and can only be overcome by the examination of new texts and the comparison of numerous passages.

A. H. SAYCE.

Queen's College, Oxford, April, 1875.

ASSYRIAN GRAMMAR.

SYLLABARY.

The characters of the Assyrian Syllabary were originally hieroglyphics, representing objects and ideas. The words by which these were denoted in the Turanian language of the Accadian inventors of the cuneiform system of writing became phonetic sounds when it was borrowed by the Semitic Assyrians, though the characters could still be used ideographically as well as phonetically. When used ideographically the pronunciation was, of course, that of the Assyrians.

In the following table only the forms of the characters found on the majority of the Assyrian monuments are given. Sometimes the so-called Hieratic characters were employed (e.g., in the Cyprian Stele of Sargon) which differ but slightly from the Babylonian. Ancient Babylonian varied again in the forms of several characters. The Elamite or Susianian characters have the same form as the ancient Babylonian, while the Protomedic are modified from the Assyrian.

The Assyrian word in the right-hand column is a translation of the Accadian word (used in Assyrian as a phonetic value) in the left-hand column, and was the sound given to the character in the Assyrian inscriptions whenever it was read as an ideograph.

Phonetic Value (Accadian word).	Cuneiform Character.	Assyrian rendering.	Meaning.
1. as	➤	magaru, dilu ...	*obedient (happy)*, ?
ruv (rum, ru)	,,	zicaru, dilu	*a male*, ?
dil	,,	nabu, dilu	*to proclaim*, ?
	,,	estin, khidu, edisu ...	*one*
	,,	namkullū	?
	,,	ina	*in*
	,,	Assur (*an abbreviation*)	*Assyria*
kharra ...	,,	samu, tuhamtu ...	*heaven, the deep*

2

Phonetic Value (Accadian word).	Cuneiform Character.	Assyrian rendering.	Meaning.
2. khal	►►	nacaśu, buligu ...	to cut, division
khas	,,	khasu	?
khal	,,	gararu	to roll stormily
	,,	pulukhu	reverence
	,,	zuzu...	a fixture
3. ?	►►►	[sumunesrit] ...	eighteen
4. an, ana ...	►►Y	sakū, samū, ilu, Anu,	high, sky, god, the god Anu
anna, annab ...	,,	sakū, samū, ilu, Anu,	high, sky, god, the god Anu
dimir, dingir...	,,	ilu	god
sa	,,	cacabu	star
essa	,,	ilutu sa sibri ...	divinity of corn
an	,,	supultu	depth
4a. nab (see 168)		nabbu	divinity
4b. simidan ...		nalbar-same... ...	the zenith
4c. alat, alap ...		sēdu	spirit (divine bull)
4d. lamma ...		lamaśśu	colossus
alap (Ass. val.)	,,	buhidu	colossus
5. khaz (khas, khats)	►×	nadu, nacaśu ...	to place, to cut
kut (kud) ...	,,	nacaśu, gazaru ...	to cut, to cut
tar	,,	nacaśu, danu, sāmu	to cut, to judge, to set
sil (śil, śila) ...	,,	sūku, panu	canal, before
gug, citamma	,,		
	,,	sallatu, halacu, eribu	spoil, to go, to descend (flow)
6. pal		ebiru, etiku, palu, napalcutu, nucuru, palu	to cross, to pass through, time or year, to revolt, enemy, sword
tal	,,	ebiru, etiku	to cross, to pass through
pal	,,	supilu sa sinnis, pukhkhu sa sinnis, supiltu	sexual part of a woman, sexual part of a woman, the lower part
nuk (?) ...	,,	nakū...	to sacrifice
zabur... ...	,,	admu, akhri, khiru ...	man, behind, lord

Phonetic Value (Accadian word).	Cuneiform Character.	Assyrian rendering.	Meaning.
7. bat, be ...	⤙	pagru, pitu, mutu, labiru, uduntu	*corpse, to open, to die, old,* ?
til, badhdhu ...	,,	gamaru, pagru, katu	*complete, corpse, hand*
us	,,	dāmu	*blood (offspring)*
khar	,,		
ziz(?), mit, idim	,,		
	,,	nakbu, samu, captu, belu, enuva, tsēru	*channel, heaven, heavy, lord, when, desert*
8. lugud ...		sarsu	*omen of good*
9. adama ...		adamatu	*omen of evil*
10. susru... ...		ussusu	*founder (surname of Anu)*
11. gir		sumuk-same, padhru	*vault of heaven, to strike*
rum	,,	littu, padhru ...	*sword, point*
gir	,,	girū, zukabulbu, padanu, birku	*point,* ?, *plain, lightning*
12. pur, pul ...		passaru	*to explain* (?)
du, gim ...	,,	edissu, sumnu ...	*alone, fat*
mucmuc-nabi	,,		
usu	,,	edisu	*solitary*
	,,	basmu, butu, macaru, garru	*sweet odour, desert* (?), *to sell* or *exchange, expedition* (?)
13. kur		naciru, sannu, pappu	*to change, enemy, other* (?)
pap	,,	pappu, zicaru, tarbu, natsaru, akhu	*other* (?), *male, young man, to defend, brother*
13a. *khal, dili-dili-nabi ...		itallucu	*a path*
gisi-u-khallacu	,,	pusku	*difficult road* (?)
14. utuci		samsu	*the Sun*
15. zubu		gamlu	*benefit*
gam	,,	sicru...	*kindness*
16. taltal... ...		Ea	*the god Hea*

Phonetic Value (Accadian word).	Cuneiform Character.	Assyrian rendering.	Meaning.
17. zicura ...		citim	*lower* or *beneath*
18. cit, cuda, se ...		epikhu, carasu ...	*to blow, property (standard, camp)*
	,,	calū, ezibu, patā ...	*the whole, to leave, to open*
śabura ...	,,	cupkhu	*?*
gudibir ...	,,	Maruducu	*Merodach*
tak	,,		
19. seslam ...		cipratu	*race* or *region*
20. ka, gita ...		... ...	determinative of measure
21. cit (kit, cat) ...		salamu	*to accomplish*
22. ru, sub ...		idu, nadanu, takku, raddu, cabadu, pakadu	*to know, to give, ?, to add, to oppress* or *be multitudinous, to oversee*
u, ub, bu ...	,,	itsbu	*?*
23. mu		sumu, santu, zicaru, nadanu, ya, samu	*name, year, memorial, to give, my, sky*
	,,	masaddu, cu'aśu, khalacu, cuśśu, vācu	*?, ?, ?, throne, ?*
nurma ...	,,		
23a. ?		idlutu	*strength*
24. nu		la, (ul), tsalamu ...	*not, image*
pateśi ...	,,	zicaru	*male (viceroy)*
25. kul (*Assyrian value* zir)		ziru	*seed*
26. zii		nūru...	*light (meteor)*
27. na		zicaru, annu, samu, makhirtu	*memorial, this, sky, front*
28. ti, til, tsil ...		baladhu, napistu, naśu	*family, life, to raise*
	,,	lakū, tsabatu, dakhu	*to take, to seize, to be near*
	,,	usibu, dapanu-sa-rucubi, anbu, tsilu	*dwell, side* (or *wheel*) *of a chariot, ?, side*

Phonetic Value (Accadian word).	Cuneiform Character.	Assyrian rendering.	Meaning.
29. uru, eri ...		ālu	a city (tent)
30. uru		ālu, abubu	city, heap of corn
31. erim		isittu	a foundation
32. sek		sakummatu	a summit
33. gur		caśamu	?
34. sacir, saciśa ...		... ...	?
35. ukki		uku, pukhru ...	people, assembly
36. uru, gisgal ... mulu		ālu, manzazu ... nisu	city, fortress man
37. silik		sagaburu	strong protector, rank
38. sucit (?) (See No. 197b.)		passuru	Lenormant "kind of parasol"
38a. kal, gar ...		?	?
39. ca, gu, cir, du, zu, cagu ...		pū, amatu, appu, pānu, inu, uznu, bunnu, makhru, sepu, amaru, amanu, kābu, sāsu, ricmu, sagamu, cibu, mātu	mouth, fealty, face, face, eye, ear, form, front, foot, sight, completion, to speak, ?, push, ?, mass, country (properly face of the country)
duk	"	ilu sa napkhari, erisu	god of the universe, to ask
gu, cagu ...	"	calu, saku ṣa me, canicu	all, drinking of water, seal
ca	"	ricim, sunnu, idculu	blow, a half, confidence (?)
39a. duddhu ...		dabibu, pālu, idacculu	deviser, ?, ?
39b. gude ...		nabu, khababu, na-gagu	proclaimer, lover (?), ?
39c. śidi, śiśi ...		urrikhtu	?

Phonetic Value (Accadian word).	Cuneiform Character.	Assyrian rendering.	Meaning.
39d. cimmu ...		sipru, dhemu ...	explanation, law
40. me		takhatsu	battle
41. impar ...		... ...	glory (name)
42. emi		lisānu ... , ...	tongue (language)
43. ?		saptu	lip (sentence)
44. ?		saptu, tsumu ...	lip, thirst
45. ? ... , ...		tsumu	thirst (fast)
46. cu		acalu, khadhdhu ...	to eat, food (חבט)
47. mû		camu	to burn (?)
48. ?		pukhkhu	the breath
49. ?		tsalamtu	darkness
50. ibira		damkaru (of Acc. origin)	?
51. ?		ikhimu	he burnt (devoured)
51a. ?		?	?
52 ?		?	?
53. ?		?	?
54. bat		imtu	poison (philtre)
55. ?		?	terror
56. ?		?	?
57. nak		satu	to drink
58. ?		uru	city
59. la		laluru, khazbu ...	?, ?

Phonetic Value (Accadian word).	Cuneiform Character.	Assyrian rendering.	Meaning.
60. tu	⊢𒂍𒁹, 𒑉𒂍𒁹	eribu, śummatu ...	*to descend* 'or *enter* or *set* (of the Sun), *season* (?)
turi, tura ...	„	eribu, murtsu ...	*to descend, &c., sickness*
61. li	⊢𒂍𒁹𒁹, ⊢𒂍𒀸, 𒑉𒀸𒁹	rāru, liliśu	?, ?
	(*note these variant forms*)		
gub, gu ...	„	illu	*high* or *precious*
ni	„		
62. apin, pin, uru	⊢𒂍𒁹	epinu, ussu	*foundation* (*city*)
engar ...	„	iccaru	*ground* (*digging*)
63. makh ...	⊢𒂍𒁹𒁹	tsiru, makhkhu (*from Acc.*), rubū, mahdu	*supreme, supreme, great, much*
	„	bahalu, tublu, tizkaru	*prince* (?), *sovereign* (?), ?
64. bar, mas ...	✦	paratsu, burru, bāru, usuru, tsindu, akhratu, akhkhuru, tsātu, rikātu, akhatu, akhu, akhitu, arcu, tsabiu	*to divide, half, half, bound, to bind, another, after, future, future, a second, brother, other, after, gazelle*
	„	camātu, gabbi, tinū, enitu, pisaktu, cabitu, mala, palaśu, tuhāmu, zibtu, dallu, ciśittu, niśu, ruzzu, elitu, śanku, makhazu, bidhru, asaridu, pulu, maru, bidhramu, ibbu, libutu, amaru, masū, vassaru, zumru, cabadtu	*heap* (?), *all, ?, ?, oracle, much, as many as, to weigh, ?, ?, the Tigris, ?, ?, ?, upper, chain, battle, firstborn* (?), *eldest, cattle, son, firstborn* (?), *white, ?, to see, ?, to abandon, body, the liver*
mas	„	māsu, Adaru, asibu, ellu, tsabitu, māzusa-ecili	?, *the god Adar, to dwell, high* (*precious*), *to take, burning* (?) *of a field*
śa	„		
65. rat, sit ...	⊢𒈨𒈨⊣	radhu	?

Phonetic Value (Accadian word).	Cuneiform Character.	Assyrian rendering.	Meaning.
66. nun		rubū, rabu, nunu, (*fr. Acc.*)	*prince, great, prince*
zil, sil, humis, khan (?)	,,		
66a. asagara ...		asagaru	*a hurricane*
67. tur, silam (?)...		tarbatsu	*rest* or *eclipse*
68. silam, akar ...		?	*reverence* (?)
69. biru (*perhaps Ass.*)		suttu, uritsu, tsiptu, nipikhu	*dream, offspring, product, revenue*
70. cun		zibbatu, zumbu ...	*tail, tail*
71. ?		?	?
72. ?		?	?
73. khu, pak ...		itstsuru, śaru ...	*bird, king* (?)
khu, pak, musen	,,	musennu	?
74. pacac ...		ciribu, sumelu ...	*middle, left hand*
75. śa		nabū	*to proclaim*
76. ik		iku (*or* ikku), daltu, khamdhu, patu, nukhsu	*?, door, quick journey, to open, prosperity*
gal	,,	basū, sacunu, nasu, labinu	*to be, placed, to raise, brick*
gal	,,	ikku, rutstsunu, malū, asabu, pitū, cānu, natsaru	*?, ?, to fill, to dwell, to open, to establish, to defend*
77. tsim, zim, nam (*Acc. prefix of abstract noun*)		simtu, sakhalu ...	*destiny, plague* (?)
nam	,,	nabu, śimmu ...	*to proclaim, destiny*
	,,	nammu, pikhatu, mā	*?, a governor, this*
78. pak (?) ...		itstsuru	*a bird*

Phonetic Value (Accadian word).	Cuneiform Character.	Assyrian rendering.	Meaning.
79. mut		banū, dāmu, uppu, aladu, icbu, biśru, barradu	to create, blood, ?, to bear children, ?, flesh, seed
musenduguśi	„		
80. zi		napistu, nisu, pilū, naśakhu, dikū, būā, saparu	life (soul), man (spirit), work, to take away, smitten, to come, to send
81. gi, śa... ...		kanū, duppu-sadhru, simtu, zicaru, mātu, eśiri, tāru, gimiru, pudak, cunu	reed, written tablet, foundation, memorial, country, bands, to restore, all, ?, established
81a. caradin ...		cissu	multitudinous
82. ?		?	?
83. ri, tal ...		tallu, ramū, lilu, tsakku, paraśu-sa-rikhuti, parsidu	mound, height, ?, ?, ?, to fly away
di	„	nabadhu	brilliance
es	„	nadū	brightness (of a star)
sa	„	saruru	the firmament
84. gub		sumelu	left hand
kat	..	gubbu (of Accadian origin)	left hand
85. tun, khub ...		khasu	?
86. pulug ...		carasu sa etsi ...	implement of wood
87. ac, gar ...		episu, banū, makharu, nabu, Nabū, kha-śiśu, pit-uzni, rap-sa-uzni, khubbu-sa-kani	to make, to build, to be present, to proclaim, Nebo, the intelligent, the opener of the ears, the enlarger of the ears, hollow of a reed
ac	„	belu...	lord
88. me		takhatsu	battle
89. sus		?	?

Phonetic Value (Accadian word).	Cuneiform Character.	Assyrian rendering.	Meaning.
90. ?		?	?
91. cum, kum ...		citu	*linen*
91a. *sa		gallabu	*sleeve* (?)
91b. sinik ...		bīnu...	?
92. ?		tsupuru	*nail (nail-mark)*
?	„	simmu	*destruction*
92a. ? ...		kharru	?
92b. sacil ...		cillu...	?
92c. tabin [or ebin], gadataccuru		tsupru, masaru, tsumbu, ubanu, imdhu	*nail, to leave* (?), *tail* (?), *peak, staff* (?)
93. dim, tim, tiv, tī		ricśu, riciś-kanē, marcaśu, timmu	*bond, bundle of reeds, cable, rope*
94. mun (munu)...		dhabtu	*benefit*
95. pulug (*from Assn.*)		pulugu	*division* or *choice*
96. en		belu, enu	*lord, lord*
	„	adi	*up to*
enu	„	samu	*sky*
97. dara ...		ṭurakhu	*antilope*
	„	Ea	*the god Ea*
98. mu		sumu	*name*
99. sur (zur) ...		zamaru, zarakhu, tsaruru, naśakhu - sa - amati, ridu, khabsu, capalu, zunnu, summa, basu	*to make go forth, to rise, body* (or *rising*), *removal of anything, servant, trodden down* (?), ?, *rain, thus, to exist*
100. sukh (śukh)		pultu, mātu, naparcu, zimu, pallu, nasaku, tihamtu	?, *country, to break, glory,* ?, *to climb, the sea*
tiskhu ...	„	ramcuti	*herd* [or *stay* ?]

Phonetic Value (Accadian word).	Cuneiform Character.	Assyrian rendering.	Meaning.
101. śucus		Istar.	the goddess Istar
102. se, sakh(śakh), nakh, nikh		surbu	prince
103. ba		episu, banū, zuzu, ciśu, nasaru, esiru, su, pitu	to make, to create, to fix, a sword, ?, a shrine, he, to open
104. zu, la		lamadu, raddu, idū, mudu, ca, nindanu	to learn, to add, to know, wise, thy, a gift
104a. abzu		abzū	the abyss
105. śu, sir		zumuru, tsuru, masacu, rabā	a body, ?, skin, to increase
106. sun (śun)		gablu	front (middle, battle)
107. muk		muccu	a building
107a. mukmuk-nabi		basmu	altar of incense
108. zadim		śaśinu	plant (?)
109. nit (nitakh, nita), eri		zicaru, ardu	man, slave
110. idu, itu		arkhu	month
111. sakh, sukh		damaku, dabu, sakhu	prosperous, a bear, tiger
112. sibir		sibru, kharpu	corn, crop
113. gur		tāru, śacibu, basu, nacru-sa-amati	to restore, ?, to be (become), breaker of faith
114. dar ... dar, śi-gunū		tarru, birmi, atsu ... litu, sutruru, pitsu ...	?, variegated cloths, growth offspring, white, white
115. ?		?	"flask, languishing" (M. Lenormant)

Phonetic Value (Accadian word).	Cuneiform Character.	Assyrian rendering.	Meaning.
116. śa, pa ...		latnu, masadu, markaśu, bu'anu	?, ?, *firmament (bond)*, *ulcer*
[śa-gitu] ...	,,		
117. gis (?) ...		samu	*the sky*
118. śi		karnu, malu, giru, enisu, śamu, issaccu, dussu, itanu, pitu, cunnu, samu	*horn, to fill, enemy (or campaign), man, blue, prince, ?, ?, to open, established, sky*
śig	,,	malū...	*to fill (give)*
118a. śicca ...		atudu	*he-goat*
119. śa'ib ...		'urukhkhu	*road*
120. śi, (śe) (*sometimes confused with dar*)		gunnu, calu, pilū, pilutu, bitru, atsu-sa-etsi-u-kani	*garden, entrails (kidneys), choice, choice, ?, growth of trees and grass*
121. mā		elippu	*a ship*
122. uz, mus ...		enzu...	*goats' hair*
123. ** ur ...		calū naccalu ...	*a complete vessel*
124. ticul, dellu ... dimśun		sukkullu, acū ...	*intelligence, ?*
125. surru ...		surrū, calū	*beginning (?), vessel*
126. guana ...		kablu	*middle*
127. ?		eratu	*pregnant*
128. dir		adru, khalabu, sutruru, khibu, mikid-isati	*dark, white, covered, wanting, burning of fire*
śa	,,	śamu	*blue*
pir	,,	saku-sa-nisi	*head of a man*
dak	,,	nikhabbu, malu, ikubbu	*covering, to fill, vault*
129. maś, (alat)		tsabu, alapu ...	*soldier, warrior spirit (bull)*

Phonetic Value (Accadian word).	Cuneiform Character.	Assyrian rendering.	Meaning.
130. sak (ris *in Ass.*)		risu, karnu, śangu, panu, rabu, avilu, pukhu	*head, horn, chain, face, great, man, ?*
130*a*. sakus ...		saku-sa-risi, asaridu...	*top of the head, eldest*
130*b*. eśśat ...		?	?
131. mukh ...		mukhkhu	*brain* (?)
132. ?		?	?
133. uru		zicaru	*male*
134. aru		nestu	*female*
135. gudhu ...		karradu	*hero*
136. can		adaru, adirtu ...	*dark, eclipse*
137. tab (tap) ...		tsabatu, tamakhu, ezibu, sitenu, uraddu, tabbu	*to seize, to hold, to leave, double* (?), *to add* (*give back*), *double*
dili-dili-nabi	„	surru, napkharu ...	*beginning, totality*
138. rū (ra) ...		banu	*to make*
kak	„	episu, cala	*to make, all*
	„	siccatu, rapdu ...	*door* (?), ?
dū, gag (*sometimes in Ass.* cal)	„	banu, danu ...	*to create, to judge*
139. ni, ne ...		yahu [*or* i]	*to be* (?)
zal (zalli), ili	„	yahu...	*to be* (?)
	„	akhkhuru, namaru, masu, zicaru, azalu, narabu, nākhu, sunku-sa-niz. ciśallu	*presence, to see, week* (?), *man, to depart,* ?, *to rest* (?), *want of* *, *altar*
140. ili		imin nabi	?
141. ir		salalu	*to spoil*
sucal ...	„	sucallu	*fruit*

Phonetic Value (Accadian word).	Cuneiform Character.	Assyrian rendering.	Meaning.
142. mal, ma, e ... gal, gā, piśannu		bitu, sacanu ...	house, to establish
ilba ...	„	saracu, maru, callu ...	to give, young, to restrain
143. gusur ...		gusuru, idiu... ...	beam, hero
144. cisal ...		ciśallu	altar
145. ?		?	?
146. nen, lucu, ekhi		ummu	mother
ismal ...	„	rapsu	large
147. ?		ummu	mother
148. gapi... ...		?	?
149. ?		alittu	generatrix
150. ega		agu	crown
151. ?		remu	mercy
152. ?		remu	grace
153. gan (gana) gāgunū		iclu, padanu, ginu, nabadhu	field, plain, enclosure (garden), light
gāgunū ...	„	khaśaśu	intelligent (to determine)
car	„	sapalu, caru... ...	lower, fortress
aganateti ...	„	nasū...	to raise
154. dak... ...		napaldhu, rapadu ...	to survive, ?
bara (par) ...	„	sutruru, adannu ...	covered, a season
155. ciśim, zibin, surin, sarin		ciśimmu, nabbillu, tsatsiru, sīkhu	different kinds of locusts
kharub (from Ass.)	„	kharubu, zirbabu ...	a locust, do.
156. agan, ubir ...		tulu, tsirtu	a mound, tent (?)
157. amas, śubura		śuburu	darkness

Phonetic Value (Accadian word).	Cuneiform Character.	Assyrian rendering.	Meaning.
158. us, nita, nitakh, dhūcus ...		emidu, zicaru, ridu, mutstsu, nitakhu, isaru, rikhu, abadu	*to stand, man, servant, offspring, man, phallus, smell*(?), ?
159. kas		sinātu	*urine*
160. tak		abnu, saku-sa-icli ...	*stone, top of a field*
161. tik, gū ...		makhru, mekhitstu, cisadu, mātu, napkharu	*front, battle, neighbourhood (bank), country, totality*
161a. izcun ...		etsen-tsiru	*tip of the tail*
161b. muśup ...		nasu-sa-resi, saku-sa-resi	*lifting of the head, top of the head*
162. gun		biltu	*tribute (a talent)*
163. dhur (dur) ...		karnu	*a crescent*
164. ?		eru	*copper*
165. hubisega ...		Bilu	*Bel*
166. sana (sa) (*read irba in Ass.*)		irbu	*four*
167. ab (ap, abba) es		abtu, esu, tamtu ... bitu, kabu	?, ?, *the sea* *house, hollow* (?)
168. nab (nap) (*see* 4a)		nuru	*light*
169. mul, ana-essecu		caccabu, nabadhu ...	*star, brightness*
170. tak (tag), sum, nas sum ... ... tak, suridu ...		labanu, libitu, lapatu, bāru, naclu dabakhu ... ... zuhunu, labatsu, makhatsu-sa-ali, śalatsu, bāru, sālu, nabatsu, nadu	*brick, omen, hinge* (?), *lake* (?), *complete* *to cut the throat* (sacrifice) *plenty* (?), ?, *stronghold of a city*, ?, *lake* (?), ?, ?, *situated*

Phonetic Value (Accadian word).	Cuneiform Character.	Assyrian rendering.	Meaning.
171. cā	 𒂍𒋛	bābu	*gate*
172. az (ats, aś) ...	 𒂍𒍝	atsu	?
173. uk (ug) ...	 𒂍𒀕	immu [*or* tammu], ucu	*day* [*or paragon*], *great* (?)
174. um, mus ... dikh ... dub, dib (duppa)	𒂍𒐈, 𒂍𒐉 " "	ummu, lību, dabacu abnu, canacu-sa-abni lāvu, dippu, tsabatu, lavū, sapacu, tabacu, saraku, tuppu, tsipu	?, ?, *to cleave to stone, signet tablet, document, to seize, to approach, to heap up, to heap up, to be red* (?), ?, *produce* (?)
175. śumuk ...	 𒂍𒈾𒐉	sūtu	*library* (?)
176. śamak ...	 𒂍𒈾𒁾	mutstsatu	*library*
177. urud (urudu)	 𒂍𒌓	eru	*bronze*
178. Ninua (?) ...	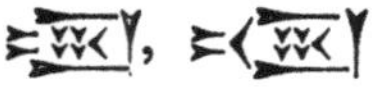 𒂍𒄩, 𒂍𒄩	Ninua	*Nineveh* (literally *bronze fish*)
179. i, i-gittū ... khi	𒄿 "	nahidu, naku, atsu-sa-samsi khu	*clear* (*glorious*), *pure, sunrise glorious* (?)
180. gan, can (kan) kam ...	𒃷 "	annu, nagabu, basu, su, khagalu *	*cloud* (?), *canal, to be, he* (*this*), *to irrigate* forms ordinal numbers
181. ad (at) ...	𒀜	abu	*father* (*king*)
182. tsi	�ad𒒳	martu	*west* (?)
183. ya	𒅀	naku	*pure*
184. tur ... ... dū	𒍗 "	zakhru, maru, karradu ablu, maru	*small, young, young warrior son, son*
185. ginna, khibiz	𒁷	muniru	*overwhelmer*
186. ibila (*borrowed from Ass.*)	 𒌉𒁽	ablu	*son*

Phonetic Value (Accadian word).	Cuneiform Character.	Assyrian rendering.	Meaning.
187. turrak ...		bintu, martu ...	*daughter, woman*
188. turrak ...		bintu	*daughter*
189. dumugu ...		samsu	*the sun-god*
190. ta, nas (*See* 205)		ina, ultu	*in, from*
191. ?		iclitu	*darkness (prison)*
192. in		innu, biltu, śilu, pillu	*lord (?), mastery, rock (?), ?*
193. un-gal, lu-gal sar (*borrowed from Ass.*)		śarru, śaru	*king, monarch*
194. rab, raba (rap) dim ...		rabbu	*?*
195. dim... ...		macutu, labartu ...	*a path (?), a phantom*
196. cib (cip, kip)		?	?
197. bi, cas (kas), ul		sane, sannu, su, suâtu, nakbu	*two, second, he, this, channel*
cas	,,	câsu (*borrowed from Acc.*)	*double*
197*a*. kharran ...		khammu	*a quarter of the sky (point of the compass)*
197*b*. sucit (?) ...		passuru	*royal parasol (?)*
198. ?		kharatsu	*to make*
199. cas (kas), ras		kharranu (durgu), sane, rabadhu	*road, two, ?*
kharran ... cas-cal ...	,, ,,	kharranu (*from Acc.*)	*road*
200. illat... ...		illat	*?*
201. rutu ...		rutu	*troops*

3

Phonetic Value (Accadian word).	Cuneiform Character.	Assyrian rendering.	Meaning.
202. gur ... ... ninda ...		namandu ... ... ittū	*measure* (?) *a sign*
203. ?		?	*" abundance, generosity "* (Lenormant)
204. is (iśi), mil, mis śakhar ...		sadu, urru ... ... 'ipru, bissatu ... summa	*mountain* (*heap*), *light* *dust, mud* *thus* (*if*)
205. ? (*See* 190)		?	*" to begin "* (Lenormant)
206. rim, cabar, im		sulū, sanu(tu) ...	*mound, seconde*(?)
207. sim, rik, śiriz		sammu	*price* (*income*)
208. ?		?	?
208. ?		nacmu	*a captive*
209. ku, kum, ri ...		saku, khasalu ...	*top, to destroy*
210. ur		isittu, cipśu-sa-nisi, uzunu, udlu	*foundation* (*the nadir*), *testicle, equal weight, level ground*
211. il, cacaśiga ...		?	?
212. du (dun) ...		alacu, alacu-khamdhu, tabalu - khamdhu, licu - khamdhu, alacu-maru	*to go, a swift journey, a swift onset, a swift march, a little journey*
gub		nazazu	*to fix* (*to wax* of the moon)
gin, aradupū		nazuzu, basu, alacu, cānu, saparu, magaru, anacu	*to be fixed, to exist, to go, to establish, to send, to love, I*
sa, ra, ir, gubba		aradubū ... ... tsabatu, sapiru, calu, sulū	*pursue* (?) *to seize, messenger, all, mound*

Phonetic Value (Accadian word).	Cuneiform Character.	Assyrian rendering.	Meaning.
212a. aradudu-nabi		cānu, uzuzu, ceśu-sa-elappi, alacu-sa-cissati	to establish, fix, pain of the womb, marching of a multitude
213. gum, nitakh		rabu, nisu ...	an official, a man
214. **r ...		? ...	"to adhere" (Lenormant)
215. rim ...		iśdu, sulu ...	foundation, heap
216. rik, khil ...		? ...	?
217. gesdin ...		caranu ...	goat [or vine]
218. ib (ip) ...		gablu, su, agagu ...	middle, he, ?
tum (tuv, tu)	"	khardatu ...	fear
urugal, aralli	"	mitu ...	death (Hades)
219. egir ...		arcu (arcatu) ...	after
aba ...	"		
220. paz (?) ...		'imiru ...	beast (ass), homer (a measure)
221. gis, nen (?) ...		etsu, zicaru, rabu, esiru	tree (wood), man, great, temple
iz (itz, iś) (Ass. value)	"		
gis ...	"	samu ...	heaven
221a. gudhu ...		caccu, tugultu, bilu, gudhu	weapon, service (servant), lord, end
221b. alal ...		alallu, miśu, metsu ...	papyrus, ?, shoot (?)
222. pa, du (?) ...		aru, gappu, gisdaru ...	?, wing, ?
khut, khat, cun	"	nahru-sa-yumi ...	dayspring
222a. luga		surupu ...	burnt
222l. gistar, tirtar		tirtu, śuśaccu ...	form (body), ?
223. pu		graphic variant of sign	

3*

Phonetic Value (Accadian word).	Cuneiform Character.	Assyrian rendering.	Meaning.
224. mar, nikh ...	𒈥	marru, sacanu, migganu, pada, radu, basu	*path, to establish, enclosure, ?, descent, to exist*
225. ge, cit ...	𒄀	citu. zacicu	*below, abyss*
lil	,,	cītu	*below*
226. hu (u), sam	𒄭	umu, ammatu ...	*the same, a cubit*
cus	,,	akhu, acalu	*brother (?), to eat*
227. ga, gur ... (*forms adjectives in Accadian*)	𒂵	gu, tsarapu, tsamadu-sa-narcabti, ma-caru - sa - macuri, sizbu	*?, purifier, chariot-yoke, cord for wares, ?*
227a. ili	𒂵 𒄑	nasu, saku, makhru, guru	*to raise, top, front, ?*
228. lakh (lakhkha)	𒇕	miśu	*?*
lakh, lukh, śun	,,	pasisu, ardu... ...	*?, servant*
succal, lukh nakh (*in Susian*)	,, ,,	succallu	*intelligence (messenger)*
229. al	𒀠	allu	*?*
230. mis (miz), rid, lak	𒈫	idlu, karā, śangu, cirbannu	*hero, to call, chain, gift*
cisip ...	,,	rittu	*?*
sit (siti) ...	,,	alittu, madadu, min utu, sadhru	*genetrix, to measure, number, to write*
ak	,,	idku	*ring (?)*
alal, piśan ...	,,	piśannu, natsabu-sa-etsi	*papyrus, shaft of a tree*
231. alal, dibbi-sak	𒁾	natsabu-sa-kani, duppu-sadhru	*shaft of a reed, written tablet*
sak	,,	Nabū	*the god Nebo*
232. gut (gud), khar, dapara, lē	𒄞	alpu, lū	*bull, herd*
telal	,,	ecimmú	*bull-like demon*

Phonetic Value (Accadian word).	Cuneiform Character.	Assyrian rendering.	Meaning.
233. cus, billudu		billudū	?
garza ...	,,	partsu	*captain (law)*
234. mascim ...		rabitsu	*an incubus*
235. sabra ...		sabru	?
236. nuzcu ...		nuscu	*Nuscu* (identified with *Nebo*)
237. sib (śiba) ...		ri'u, belu	*shepherd, lord*
238. sab (sap), gis-tar-urassa-cu		sabbu, gablu, saramu	*?, interior, to sacrifice*
239. e		kābu, bitu, kabu ...	*hollow, house, to speak*
240. duk ...		sacunu	*a building*
lut	,,	pulgu, carpatu ...	*choice, ?*
241. un		nisu	*man*
ucu	,,	uku (*from Acc.*) ...	*people*
calama ...	,,	matu	*country*
241. dan ...		dannu	*strong*
cal, gurus ...	,,	asdhu, akru, dannu, egiru, asaridu	*?, costly, mighty, to dig, eldest*
lab, lib, rib ...	,,	idlu	*a warrior*
gurus ...	,,	gurusu, idlu ...	*a warrior, a hero*
zan, śim ...	,,	mātu	*country*
242. am		rīmu	*wild bull*
243. uzu		sīru	*flesh (limb, health)*
244. ne, iz ...		isatu, napakhu ...	*fire, to dawn*
bi, bil, pil, gibil	,,	kalū	*to burn*
dhe ...	,,	cararu, essetu, sussu	*to revolve, new, sixty*
cum (*of Ass. origin*)	,,	camu	*to burn*

Phonetic Value (Accadian word).	Cuneiform Character.	Assyrian rendering.	Meaning.
245. gi, gibil ...	𒀭	kalū, bu'idu... ...	*to burn, a spirit*
246. gil, śim ...	𒀭	?, idguru	*"construction, wall, to glide"* (Lenormant)
247. guk	𒀭	cibuśu, garru, mandinu	*trampling, expedition, gift* (?)
248. nir	𒀭	śarru, malicu ...	*king, prince*
249. acar ...	𒀭	aplukhtu	*reverence*
250. ub (up), ār (ara)	𒀭	cipru, tupku, garmu, enakhu	*region, zone, quarter, to decay*
251. mebulug (*of Ass. origin*)	𒀭	mebulugu, sabuccu...	*choice,* ?
252. gab, dū, takh	𒀭	makharu, irtu, daku, padharu, padi, isi, dakhadu, nadhalu, naśikhu, etsibu, saninu, nadhalu	*front, breast, to strike, to deliver,* ?, *he has, to rejoice, to raise, a remover, to establish, a rival, to transfer*
takh ...	,,	labanu-libanu ...	*brickwork*
	,,	radu	*descent* (or *thunderbolt*)
253. zin	𒀭	tseru	*desert*
zer (*of Ass. origin*)	,,		
rabita ...	,,	iztati	?
254. takh ...	𒀭	etsibu, uraddu ...	*to establish, to dispose*
255. sam ...	𒀭	sīmu	*price*
256. zik (zig), khas	𒀭	zikku, sabru, garru ...	?, *to break, expedition* (?)
257. uru	𒀭	aru, epuru	?, *fecundity*
ugudili ...	,,	esgurru	?
258. ?	𒀭	?	?

Phonetic Value (Accadian word).	Cuneiform Character.	Assyrian rendering.	Meaning.
259. usbar …		uspa-rabu … …	*great quiver*
uzu'… …	„	barū… … …	*?*
260. urugal …		gabru … …	*opposer (hero)*
261. sam… …		? … … …	*?*
262. aca … …		rāmu, nasu, madadu, maharu	*high, to raise, to measure, to urge on*
ram (*Ass. value*)	„		
263. ? … …		partsu … …	*divider (?)*
264. lab, rud …		alu … … …	*city*
265. agarin …		ummu … …	*mother (?)*
266. ? … …		śarru … …	*king*
267. ubigi …		? … … …	*shrine (?)*
268. ? … …		? … … …	*?*
269. gaz (gaza), bi		dāku, niku, puhuz, khibu	*to smite, victim, ?, wanting (?)*
270. lil, ubi … galam, galum		abutu, śaru, naclu …	*charm, king, complete*
271. ? … …		? … … …	*?*
272. zicura …		irtsitu … …	*the earth*
273. taltal …		Ea … … …	*the god Ea*
274. śi, se, sem …		nadanu, sacaru …	*to give, to give*
	„	nadu, śapanu, idu, sāmu, palaśu	*to place, to sweep away, to lay, to set, to weigh (be favourable)*
śi, śunnu …	„	ananu-sa-*, lavu-sa-*	*?, tablet of**

Phonetic Value (Accadian word).	Cuneiform Character.	Assyrian rendering.	Meaning.
275. rakh, ukhúla		?	?
276. śar		sadhru, muśaru, sumu	to write, an inscription, name
khir, khur ...	,,	zarakhu, zamaru, da-rudu, atsu-sa-etsi-u-kani	to rise, to dawn, ?, growth of trees and grass
khir... ...	,,	arku, raciśu, rucuśu, ciru, calū, nabu, caśu	green, to bind, bond, enclosure, all, to proclaim, to cover
cismakh, * gū	,,	samu	sky
277. ubara ...		cididu	glow (spark)
	,,	cidinu, rimutu, nira-rutu	protection (law), grace, help
278. asilal ...		risātu	eldest (first)
279. bat		dūru, mitutu ...	fortress, death
280. dadhru ...		dabibu	deviser
281. mermer ...		Rammanu	the air-god (Rimmon)
282. lū		dalakhu	to trouble
guk... ...	,,	cuccu	?
283. gā, de ...		taru, nacaru, passakhu, napalu, nakamu, ecimu, cipupi, pala-khu, calalu, saba-dhu, nacru-sa-amati	to return, to change, to pass over, to throw down, to punish, to strip, ?, to worship, to complete, staff (?), breaker of faith
284. cus		nākhu, nikhu, tsalamu	to rest, rest, shadow (eclipse)
śur, sur ...	,,	iśśu, saccagunū ...	mighty, ?
	,,	izzis, uzzis	strongly (?)
285. ra		rakhatsu, akhazu, ana, rapasu	to inundate. to take, to (for), to enlarge
sa ...	,,	lā, lū, ...	not, ?

Phonetic Value (Accadian word).	Cuneiform Character.	Assyrian rendering.	Meaning.
285. kal (?) ...		cipru	region (race)
286. uśan ...		?	?
286a. ?	(in Pers. Insc.)	napalcutu	rebel
287. sa, gum, cū, mulu, lugur, nita		nisu, avilu	man, man
287a. azalak ...		azlacu	?
287b. dinik ...		sibtsu	?
288. sis ... ... ur (uru) ...		akhu, urinnu ... natsaru, nuru	brother, peacock to help, light
289. da [individualising affix in Acc.]		pidnu, nasū-sa-nisi ... pidhnu	field (furrow), top of a man yoke
290. zak (śak), zik		zaggu, amutu, ebiltu, adi, isaru, idu, itatu, pūlū, bircu, atsidu, isdu, bamatu, tsēru, emuku, asaridu, sumelu, ricśu, pādu	?, true (?), lordship, up to, just (straight), house, wall, cattle, knee, ?, heap, high place, supreme, deep, eldest, left hand, bond (building), frontier
tami .. zikkad ...	” ”	simtu	destiny
291. ma, mamū ...		sacanu, padinnu, mātu zacaru	to dwell, plain, country to commemorate
292. as		arratu, ciccinu, tsibutu, khasakhu, madadu	curse (enchantment), ?, wish, want, to measure
dessu ...	”	samu	heaven
293. gal, [tak in Susian.]		gallu, rabu	great, great
293a. utaccal ...		utaccilu	?
293b. ulad ...		dabikhu	?

Phonetic Value (Accadian word).	Cuneiform Character.	Assyrian rendering.	Meaning.
293c. kigal ...	𒂅𒀭	muhirru	*ruler*
294. ?	𒂅	karū...	*to invoke*
295. mir, ega ...	𒂅	agu, banu, uzzu ...	*crown (halo), tiara, coronet*
dhun-gunū ...	„	śibbu, śibkhū, iltanu	*girdle, turban* (Heb. מספחת), *north* (?)
296. bar (bara) ...	𒁇, 𒁇	paraccu, basamu, udu, risku	*altar (sacrifice), balsam, aloe, nard*
sar (sara) ...	„	sāru, paraccu ...	*incense* (?), *altar*
297. bur, gul (?), ninda-gunū	𒀫	isdu, būru, śalatu-sa-*, abnu	*heap, ?, ?, stone*
298. bis (pis), cu'a-gunū	𒂅	cu'a-gunū, palakhu, rapadu, mamluv, khuzabu, salalti, napasu	*Merodach of the garden* (?), *to worship, ?, rain, clay* (?), *spoiling, to stretch*
kir (cir), gar	„	cabattu	*liver*
299. gar, kar ...	𒃻	abbuttu, karru ...	*?, ?*
300. pir	𒃻	?	*?*
301. id	𒃻	idu, ikhitu, cuśśu ...	*hand (power), one (fem.), throne* [the character seems originally to have denoted a *comb*]
a	„	karnu	*horn*
302. ?	𒂊	paratsu	*to speak falsely*
303. uru, muru ...	𒂊	gablu	*the middle (battle)*
unu ...	„	nasacu, niku, subtu, biru	*to pour out, libation, seat, ?*
304. de	𒂊	saku-sa-ikli, sicitu, tupuku, nas'u	*top of a field, surface* (?), *district, to tcar up (remove)*
śi, idgal ...	„	nappakhu	*to dawn*
umun ...	„	mummu	*?*
ubil ...	„	sagumu	*?*

Phonetic Value (Accadian word).	Cuneiform Character.	Assyrian rendering.	Meaning.
305. ?		?	" *hermaphrodite*" (Oppert)
306. lil		lillu	*sorcery* (?)
307. śukh, lukh ...		tsabatu, ri'u, tallicu ...	*to seize, shepherd, a march*
308. ?		pulu...	*cattle*
309. alam, alala, bi-seba		tsalamu	*image*
lani, sabaru	,,	bunnu	*image* (*sculpture*)
310. bisebi ...		samsu	*the sun*
311. khilip ...		ilu	*god*
312. ?		belatu	*lady*
313. śik, śizi, ara...		arku, urcitu... ...	*green, verdure*
	,,	banu	*old gazelle*
314. dub... ...		napatsu, egu ...	*to break in pieces, to surround*
balag ...	,,	balangu	*division*
bamiś ...	,,		
315. sa		lu	?
nā	,,	pidhnu	*yoke*
316. accada, bur-bur		tilla, saki	*highland* (**Accad**), *the summits*
317. su, sugab, kat		katu, idu, gimillu, emuku, ubanu	*hand, hand* (*power*), *benefit, hollow, peak*
317*a*. khul (?) ...		nigū, gamalu ...	*control* (?), *to benefit*
317*b*. tucundi ...		summa	*thus* (*if*)
318. curu ... (*See No.* 111.)		damiku	*prosperous*

Phonetic Value (Accadian word).	Cuneiform Character.	Assyrian rendering.	Meaning.
319. sâ ...	𒀭 𒀭, 𒀭 𒀭	damaku	*fortunate*
gisimmar ...	”	gisimmaru	*?*
320. lab, lul, ruk, nar, rar, pakh, lib	𒀭	śarru	*king*
320. se	𒀭, 𒀭	seum, ziru, ittu, amaru, magaru	*corn (grain), seed, wheat, wheat, happy*
niga ...	”	marū	*young*
sana, sananabacu	”	irbittu ... ... ?	*four* *hin (a measure)*
321. bu (pu), śir, gid	𒀭, 𒀭	śēru, sadadu, ericu, nūru	*?, long, to extend, light*
sepuz ...	”	maru, naśakhu, rabadu, ebiru	*young, to remove, to adorn (?), to cross*
śus, guz ...	”	napakhu, Davcina ...	*to dawn, the goddess Daukê*
322. ?	𒀭	?	*?*
323. sud	𒀭𒀭, 𒀭𒀭	ericu, rukutu ...	*to extend, distant*
śu	”	śir-gunu	*?*
ezu	”	arū, zaraku, śulukhu, irisu, sakhalu	*?, bucket (?), pardon (?), request (?), plague (?)*
324. tsir (śir) ...	𒀭𒀭, 𒀭𒀭	tsiru...	*serpent*
mus... ...	”	musu	*serpent (?)*
325. uz (uts, uś), śir	𒀭𒀭, 𒀭𒀭	uśu, tsiru	*?, serpent*
326. tir	𒀭𒀭, 𒀭𒀭	cisatu (kistu), dayanu,	*jungle, judge*
327. te, dimmenna	𒀭	temennu, tsabatu, cuśśu	*floor (foundation-stone), to seize, throne*
te, dikh (of Ass. origin)	”	dakhu	*to face*
327a. mulla ...	𒀭 𒀭	?	*?*
327b. unu, temenes-gunū	𒀭 𒀭	maca *	*

Phonetic Value (Accadian word).	Cuneiform Character.	Assyrian rendering.	Meaning.
328. car	𒋼	caru, ediru, ecimu, dakhu	*fortress, to arrange, to strip, to face*
329. u	‹	belu, śaru, ubanu, śilu	*lord, king, peak, rock*
pur, bur ...	„	esritu, suplu ...	*ten, below*
ge	„	mikhiltu	*battle*
umun ...	„	damu	*blood (offspring)*
330. babar ...	‹𒁹	putstsū-sa-kan-dubba	*white surface to receive an inscription*
331. si, lim (liv, li)	‹𒁹	enu, amaru, makharu	*eye, to see, before (witness)*
	„	panu, igu	*presence (face), ?*
	„	mātu, ecitsu ...	*country, ?*
ir (?), tim (?)	„		
332. khul ...	‹𒁹	kullulu, limuttu, khumkhum	*accursed (evil), baneful, sultry*
333. curuv ...	‹𒁹	pakadu, damku ...	*overseer, propitious (of good omen)*
334. seba, izcu (?)	‹𒁹	tugultu, ardutu, libittu	~~service, servitude, omen~~
335. ?	‹𒁹	?	*(astronomical) observation*
336. pam (pav, pā)	‹𒁹	zacaru, nabu, tamatu, namru, utu	*to remember, to proclaim, ?, bright, ?*
337. ar	‹𒁹	?	?
338. ?	‹𒁹	nemicu	*deep wisdom*
339. va	‹𒁹	u, naku, śarru ...	*and, to sacrifice, king*
tsi	„		
340. timkhir ...	‹𒁹 ‹𒁹	Nabiuv	*the god Nebo*
341. pikh ...	‹𒁹	?	?

Phonetic Value (Accadian word).	Cuneiform Character.	Assyrian rendering.	Meaning.
342. di, dim ...	〈⧸⊨⧸, ⧽⧾	dēnu (dīnu), salamu, śulmu, erisu, sananu, sakabu, śararu, casadu	*to judge, to end, rest, to ask, to rival, to make speak, ?, to conquer*
śa	,,	milcu, śarar-śirri ...	*king (judge), ?*
śilim, sallim (*of Ass. origin*)	,,	śulmu, sulummu ...	*rest (completion, recompense), peace (alliance)*
342a. śagar, śagalum	〈⧸⊨⧸ ▽	malicu	*a king*
343. ci (cina), cicū	〈⊫⧸, 〈⊫⧸	itti (ittu), asru, kakkaru, mātu, irtsitu, saplu, asābu, anna, ema	*with, place, ground, country, earth, lower, a dwelling, on, about*
cizlukh ...	,,	mascanu	*high place*
343a. utu ...	〈⊫⧸ 〈⊫⧸	citim-sa	*below it (its lower part)*
343b. canlab ...	〈⊫⧸ ⊨⧸⧸⧸	suluv, nidutu, terictu, asru, ramanu	*high, high place, extension, place, self*
343c. siten ...	〈⊨⧸ ⊥	malacu	*to rule*
344. durud ...	⧸⊫⧸	carru	*fortress*
345. va (?), cicas (?)	〈⊨⧸⧸⧸	sū	*like (the same, ditto, repetition)*
346. cusi... ...	〈⧸⧸⊨⧸	?	*?*
347 sakkad ...	〈⊨⧸⧸⧾	cubsu, Nabiuv ...	*crown, the god Nebo*
348. lit, lat (lad)...	〈⊏	?	*?*
ab	,,	arkhu	*month*
u	,,	... ...	*... ... ...*
349. cir (kir) ...	〈⊱⧸⧸⧸	cīru, tsurru	*plantation (?), bowels*
ub	,,	ubbu	*?*
libis... ...	,,	labbu	*heart (interior)*
sem... ...	,,	khalkhallatu ...	*desire (?)*
350. metsi	〈⧸⊢⊢××	manzu	*?*

Phonetic Value (Accadian word).	Cuneiform Character.	Assyrian rendering.	Meaning.
351. ?	〈⊳- ⼻⼻ ⟨⼻⊢, 〈⊳⊳ ⼻⼻⼻ ⊢⼻⊢	ditanu	*chamois* (?)
351a. alim, sagira-cu'a-igīdu	〈⊳⊳ ⼻⼻ ⼻⊢	Bilu, śarru, Beltu, mitanu, cuśariccu	*the god Bel, king, goddess Beltis, plague*, ?
352. cis (kis) ...	〈⟨⟨⟨	cissatu	*multitude*
353. ner	〈⊨⊨	sepu	*foot (basis)*
ne, pisim ...	"	emuku	*deep*
aric ...	"	nēru, pisimmu ...	*yoke*, ?
	"	namru	*bright*
354. tidnu ...	〈⊨⊨ 〈⊨	akharru	*behind (the west)*
355. liliś	〈⊨⌐ ⊨⌐	liliśu	*barrier* (?)
356. zigarū ...	〈⊨⼻⼻ 〈⊨⼻⼻	samū	*heaven*
357. sacan (?) ...	〈⊨⊨	sacanu	*to appoint*
357. sadugacunu	〈⼻⊳<, 〈⼻	na'idu,'ublu, nakhagunmatu, parsu'hu, śaśu, mūnu, selibbū	*insect* (?), *worm*, ?, *flea, moth, worm, worm*
dūgu ...	"	bircu, dābu, rikhu ...	*knee, good, odour* (or *breath*)
358. gingir ...	〈⼻⼻	Istar	*the goddess Istar*
359. amar ...	〈⼻	buru, gannu	*light* (?), *enclosure*
zur (*of Ass. origin*)	"	... ...	... ...
360. sigisse ...	〈⼻⼻	niku, taslu, ciribu ...	*victim, prayer, offering*
361. nim, num, nū	〈⼻	saku, elamu, zību ...	*top, highland (Elam), wolf*
enum (enuv)	"	samū	*heaven*
	"	nakaru - sa - semiri, garru, zumbu	*cutting by means of the diamond,* ?, *a fly*
362. zum ...	〈⼻⼻⼻	napalu	*to destroy*

Phonetic Value (Accadian word).	Cuneiform Character.	Assyrian rendering.	Meaning.
363. tum... ...	〈𒄑𒌝〉	babalu	*to bring down (produce)*
364. lam (lav) ...	〈𒇽〉	lammu	*a seat (?)*
365. nū	〈𒇻〉	rabatsu	*to rest*
366. nā	〈𒈿〉	udhalu (utalu) ...	*eclipse (setting)*
gud ...		rabatsu, nadu, mayalu	*to lie down, to settle, bed*
367. ul, dū, udbu- guddhu	〈𒌌〉	cacabu	*star*
ru	„	elipu - sa - etsi, śumu, surru, calulu, tac-cabu, muttacbu	*ship of wood, ?, ?, ?, point˚ (?), pointer (?)*
368. cir (kir) ...	〈𒅕〉	śalkhu (?)	*citadel*
369. bam, ban, bav	〈𒁀〉	mitpanu, kastu ...	*bow, bow*
370. dim, sitimmu	〈𒁴〉, 〈𒁴〉	cima, summa, banu, episu, basū, sama-dhu, matsū	*like, thus, to form, to make, to be, ?, to find*
tum (tuv)	„	banu, kharatsu, khar-tsu	*to produce, to create, ob-scurity*
cim, gim (*of Ass. origin*)	„	... ...	... ...
	„	idinnu	*?*
371. sita	〈𒋡〉	ricśu, patlulu ...	*bond, mixed (?)*
372. * ruv ...	〈𒆠〉	cīrū	*?*
373.	〈𒂊〉	*?*	*?*
374. mi, vi, gig, cu	〈𒈪〉	tsalmu, eribu ...	*shade (black), sunset*
ge	„	musu	*night*
cuga ...	„		
375. śun	〈𒋜〉	nardapu	*pursuit (?)*
gul (kul) ...	„	abatu	*to destroy*
	„	subtu, calu-sa-avili ...	*seat, whole of a man*

Phonetic Value (Accadian word).	Cuneiform Character.	Assyrian rendering.	Meaning.
376. dugud ... cab (*Ass. value*)	〈𒐕〉, 〈𒐕〉 "	cabdu, miktu ...	*heavy (much, honor), ?*
377. gig ...	𒄰	martsu, śimmu, cibtu	*sick, plague, affliction*
378. din (tin) ... gal	𒁷, 𒈹 "	baladhu ... ... bitu	*life (family)* *house*
379. ugun ...	𒌋	akhzētu, Naná ...	*?, the goddess Nana*
380. mukh ...	𒈾	mukhkhu, eli, banu, alidu	*over, over, to create, to beget*
381. caccul ...	𒆰, 𒆰	kakkullu, namzitu ...	*?, ?*
382. man, in, nis buśur ... śar (*Ass. value*)	𒎙 "	śaru ... ... samsu, esrā	*king* *the sun, twenty*
383. cus (cusu) ...	𒐏	pulu...	*cattle*
384. es ... ... esseb ... śin (*Ass. value*)	𒐐 " "	bitu ... ... salasā, Śinu ...	*house* *thirty, the Moon*
385. sanabi ...	𒐗	irbahā	*forty*
386. usu	𒌋	erib-samsi	*sunset*
387. nigin ...	𒌋 𒐊	cummu	*the interior of the earth*
388. lagar ...	𒋻	lagaru	*?*
389. cizlukh (?) ...	𒆳	mascanu	*high*
390. tul (dhul) ...	𒌇, 𒌇	bakhilu, ridu-sa-riduti, sadu	*?, harem, hill*
dul	"	catamu	*to conceal*
mul... ...	"	mulu	*?*
durud ...	"	carru	*fortress*

4

Phonetic Value (Accadian word).	Cuneiform Character.	Assyrian rendering.	Meaning.
391. cū	𒀀	ellu, caśpu	high (noble, precious), silver (money)
391a. babbar ...		caśpu	silver
391b. guski ...		khuratsu	gold
392. mun ...		idlū	a hero
393. dun... ... sul	 ,,	idlu, dannu ... ... śulum	hero, strong ?
394. eśa, śa ...		khamesserit, Istar, imnu	fifteen, the goddess Istar, right hand
395. pad (pat), kur (?) ... suk	 ,,	śimtu, sipartu ...	plague, bill (account)
396. gam (gū) ... lus, gur ...		iśacu, lanu, kanduppi, musacnis, cubuśu, kabu	to pour (?), a dwelling, a papyrus-scroll, subduer, a trampling, to speak
397. *		Sign of a division	between words or sentences
398. *		do.; also a	contracted form of the number 9
399. cur (kur) ... mat (mad) ... lat (lad), nat (nad), sat (sad) ra'er ...	 ,, ,, ,,	curu, sadu, elu, garu, nacaru, napakhu mātu, casadu ... mātu, sadu	land, mountain (the east), high, foreign, hostile, to dawn country, to conquer (acquire) country, mountain
400. ana		... ...	to root up
401. lis, dil (dul)		iddu **	?

Phonetic Value (Accadian word.)	Cuneiform Character.	Assyrian rendering.	Meaning.
402. ud (utu, ut), par		samsu, yumu, namaru, enu, nahru-sa-yumi, urru, pitsu, atsu	*sun, day, to see, eye, dawning of day, light, white, to rise*
lakh... ...	„	samsu, śarru, ellu ...	*sun, king, high*
zal (śal), tam	„	samsu	*the sun*
sam (,u) ...	„	yumu, immu, samsu	*the day, the day, the sun*
zab, erim ...	„	tsābu, bibu	*soldier (host)*
babar ...	„	tsit-samsi, namaru ...	*sunrise, to see*
402a. e		atsu, makhkhu, padu	*to rise (issue), mighty, sceptre*
402b. ukh (ukhu) (*see* 405)		cusu, ruhtu... ...	*?, poison (?)*
402c. zabar ...		śiparru	*copper (bronze)*
403. bir		nuru, namaru ...	*light, to see*
erim, lakh ...	„	tsabbu	*soldier (host)*
zab, śab (*Ass. values*)			
403a. ** nus ...		pilu	*choice*
404. ?		niraru	*helper*
405. ukh... ...		ruhtu	*poison (philtre)*
406. pi		uznu	*ear*
ā, tal, pi, me	„	me, giltanu	*water, drop*
407. 'ā, āh ...		giltanu	*drop of water*
408. sā, lib, śini ...		labbu	*heart (middle, within)*
408a. śini ...		kunkut [*or* kuntar] ...	*?*
409. pis		eru, aladu	*pregnant, begetting*
410. bir		saradhu	*paint (?)*
411. nanam ...		cinu	*established (firm)*

4*

Phonetic Value (Accadian word).	Cuneiform Character.	Assyrian rendering.	Meaning.
412. gudu ...		?	to set (end)
413. zib (śib, tsib)		zibbu	?
414. khi, khig ...	(also written)	dhābu, cissatu, esiru	good, multitude, propitious (holy)
dhi, khā ...	„	cissatu-sa-same, bircu	legions of heaven, a knee
id, sar (śar-rab), śib (zib), dhum	„	... ...	a measure
dar, dhar ...	„	pallilu, Assuru ...	to mingle, the god Assur
sar, dūgu (See No. 357)	„	cissatu, mādu, rabu, mukhudu, sutabū, dussu, nukhsu, pumalu, nakhasu-sa-nukhsi	multitude, much, great, great, ?, ?, prosperity, powerful, prosperer of prosperity
415. im		rukhu, rikhu, ramanu, palakhu, rarubatu	wind (air, tempest, cardinal point), breath, self, to worship, fear
sar	„	sāru, samu	brightness (sky), heaven
mir, muru ...	„	nahdu, irbu, Rammanu	bright, rain, the Air-god
im	„	pulukhtu, emuku, zumru	fear, deep, body (person)
imi	„	samu, irtsitu, akhu, didu, sāru, zunnu, duppu	sky, earth, brother (?), ?, brightness, rain, tablet (?)
415a. latakh ...		uduntu-sa-rukhi ...	quantity of wind
416. kam (cam), kham		... ...	denotes ordinal numbers
416a. esses ...		?	?
417. ah (h, hi) ...	, (in Persian inscriptions)	'umunu	small worm

Phonetic Value (Accadian word).	Cuneiform Character.	Assyrian rendering.	Meaning.
418. akh, ikh, ukh, (ukhu)	 𒀝	uplu, kalmatu, pursu'u, umunu	worm, vermin, flea, small worm
	"	rukhuku	distant
lammubi ...	"	nāpu	worm
419. bir	 𒁈	sapikhu	a destroyer
420. khar ...	 �	semiru, esiru ...	diamond, bracelet
mur, ur, cin, kham	"	cirbu, khasu, zumru	centre, liver, body
420a. urus (=the god Bel in Cassite)	 𒄴	tirtu, tirtu-sa-khasē ...	body (form), ?
421. khus (khuś)	 𒄷	khussu	beaten out (small gazelle)
rus	"	russu	young gazelle, blue cloth
422. śukh, śukhar	 𒄸	cimmatu	family (household)
423. zun	 𒍪	mahdutu	many
424. ?	 𒀹	belatu	lady
425. ?	 𒀺	rabu, dannu ...	great, strong
426. zicara ...	 𒍣	samu	the sky
427. dis (tis), gi ... ana (Ass. value)	𒁹	ana, śarru, estinu ...	to, king, one
	"		
428. lal	𒆷	malu, madhu, sapacu, sakalu, ubburu-sa-amati, khizu, sapalu, etsilu, śaradu-sa-cipratu, śanaku, cima, tartsu, callu, ensu	to fill, to fall (?), to pour out, to weigh (pay), crossing of the sea, ?, under (below), idle (?), ?, chain, like, facing (in the time of), to restrain, sick
nas, lū ...	"	sakalu, tsabatu, tsimdu, nīru, aniru	to weigh, to seize, yoke, yoke, yoke
429. lal, ū ...	 𒇲	sukalulu	to equal (reach)

Phonetic Value (Accadian word).	Cuneiform Character.	Assyrian rendering.	Meaning.
430. usar... ...	𒑰𒁹𒌋	settu	*bank*
431. ucu	𒑰𒌋	labnu	*brick*
432. nanga ...	𒑰𒀸	nagu (*of Acc. origin*)	*a district*
433. lalu	𒑰𒈨	libbātu	*brickwork*
434. me	𒈨	kulu, kālu, tamtsu, zicaru, takhatsu, dūtu, meh, samu	*assembly, to assemble, mass, man, battle,* ?, 100, *sky,* sign of the plural
isip, sib (sip)	„	ramcu	*herd*
435. mes (mis) ...	𒈨𒐀, 𒈨𒐀	mahdutu, libbu ...	*many, heart,* sign of the plural
436. kas, ili ...	𒈫	sinu, sanu	*two, repetition* (*ditto*)
min... ...	„		
437. 'a (*forms participles in Acc.*)	𒈫 (*also written* 𒈫𒈫)	me, abu, 'ablu ...	*water, father, son*
pur	„	nahru	*river*
dur	„	labacu	?
it	„	nāku	*pure* (*sacrifice*)
ga, e ...	„	rakipu	?
437a. eba ...	𒈫𒂠	melu	*flood*
437b. ara... ...	𒈫𒂖	milcu	*king* (or *crocodile*)
437c. ir	𒈫𒁹	dimtu, calū naccalu, unninnu	*a pile, complete vessel,* ?
437d. aria ...	𒈫𒅆	nahru	*river*
438. ai	𒈫𒈫	abu	*father*
439. ?	𒈫𒌓	iddu...	*bitumen*
440. kurnun ...	𒋼	Tasmitu	*the goddess Tasmit* (wife of Nebo)
441. za (tsa) ...	𒈫	arbu, ci, atta ...	*four, like, thou*

Phonetic Value (Accadian word).	Cuneiform Character.	Assyrian rendering.	Meaning.
141*a.* uknu ...	𒌋𒋼	ibbu...	*white*
142. kha	𒄩	nunu, ranu, simru, nabu, khalaku	*fish, ?, ?, to proclaim, to divide (destroy)*
'a, ua ...	,,	Cū'a...	*Merodach's oracle*
143. gug (guk) ...	𒄖	śamtu	*blue*
144. zakh ...	𒍝	?	?
144. ner ...	𒉌	nēr	*measure* or *space of six hundred*
145. dar, ara ...	𒁰	?	80
146. essa... ...	𒐈	salsatu ... .·.	*three*
146*a.* gar *or* sā ...	𒐊	ribu	*a fathom*
146*b.* gi (?) ...	𒃻	kanu...	*a cane (measure)*
147. sana, sa ... irba (*Ass. value*)	𒀹 ,,	irbu, ribu, nitu ...	*four, a quarter, ?*
gar	,,	episu, sacanu, saracu, girū, naśakhu-sa-tirti, rakhatsu, zaltu, nūru, khamdhu, gamalu, maśakhu, garru, sēmu, nitu, acalu, cumuru, su-cunnu, eristu	*to make (do), to dwell, to furnish, hostile, removal of body, to inundate, battle, light, speedy, to benefit, removal, food, obedient, ?, food, ?, fortress, bride (?)*
sā	,,	?, mala, nasu ...	*a measure* (a quart), *as many as, to lift up*
148. śa, para ...	𒕪	khamsa	*five*
ya, i ...	,,	nahdu	*glorious*
149. as	𒐋	sissu	*six*
150. sisna ...	𒅓	śibu	*seven*
151. ?	𒐐 , 𒐙 , 𒉽	tisu	*nine*

Phonetic Value (Accadian word).	Cuneiform Character.	Assyrian rendering.	Meaning.
452. nin		allatu	*wife*
453. ?		sumelu	*the left hand*
454. esseb ...		sarru	*king*
455. duk, tuc (tug) dū		tucu, isu, akhazu, si-mū, zarakhu, tsa-maru	*to have, to have, to possess, to place, to rise, to rise (of stars)*
456. ur		khamamu, etsidu, na-raru, aruru, khazu	*heat (celestial sphere), to hew (?), to burn, burnt, ?*
457. sussana ...		sussanu	*one-third*
457a. gigim ...		ecimmu	*demon*
458. sanibi ...		sīnibu	*two-thirds (forty)*
459. utuk ...		uduccu	*spirit*
460. kiguśili, parap		parapu	*five-sixths*
461. mascim ...		mascimmu	*a demon*
462. cu		usibu, subtu, marcaśu, ina, ana, rubū, akru, tucultu	*to sit down, seat, bondage, in, to, prince, precious, service*
iputugulacu	,,		
dur, pī, tul ...	,,	tucultu, nukhu, zacaru	*service, rest, to record*
us	,,	dhemu	*law*
zi	,,	cemu	*clothes*
tū	,,	nadu, tsubatu ...	*to place, clothes*
se	,,	tucullu	*trust (service)*
tus (dus), khun, seba, mugu, ipu-tugulacu	,,		
	,,	nasu-sa-eni, muśaru, dū, tsillu, mulū, succu, sa-subat-apzi	*raising of the eyes, inscription, ?, side, ascent (?), booth, seat of the underworld*

Phonetic Value (Accadian word).	Cuneiform Character.	Assyrian rendering.	Meaning.
463. gil, khap (khab), gur (gu), cir, (kir, gir), rim, girim, gar, zam, mik, lagab	⬜	lagabu	?
	„	racaśu, pukhkhuru, gararu-sa-nisi, śecuru, dubutu, bahalu, bihisu	*to bind, gathering, tumult of men, enclosing, ?, to fear* (?), ?
463a. puda (gidda)	⬜ 𒂊𒌗	aricu, ruku	*long, distant*
464. zar (tsar, śar)	𒍠	?	?
465. umuna ...	𒍝	alapu	*a thousand* "*festival*" (Lenormant)
466. zarip ...	𒍣	?	?
467. uh, ua ...	𒄴𒀹	rubtsu, cabasu, pikannu	*flock, sheep*
468. ?	𒋻	taccabu	?
469. suk ... ... umun ...	𒌋𒌋 „	tsutsu ... ... khammu	*aquatic plant* (*plant, marsh*) *heat* (*zone*)
470. pu ... ... pur (*See No.* 223)	𒌑, 𒀀𒌑 „	tsutsu ... ... pūru, muspalu ...	*pool* (*marsh*) *pool* (?), *low ground*
471. bul	𒌍	?	?
472. ?	𒍞	?	*a cornfield* (?)
473. ?	𒌋𒌋	?	?
474. cu (?) *or* sāgar (?)	𒅖	khusukhkhu ...	*famine*

Phonetic Value (Accadian word).	Cuneiform Character.	Assyrian rendering.	Meaning.
475. sū	𒀀	zirku	*a bucket*
476. gur	𒄢	apśu...	*running water*
zicuv ...	,,	samū	*heaven*
477. ?	𒄞	?	?
478: ?	𒅗	iddu (*see No.* 439) ...	*bitumen*
479. ?	𒄠	narcabtu	*chariot*
480. ?	𒀊	pagru	*corpse*
481. nigin ...	𒌋𒌋 (See No. 463)	napkharu, pakharu, śakharu, nagarruru, tsai'idu, tsadu-salavē, pasaru, epusu, racaśu	*collection, to collect, to surround, tumultuous assembly, hunter, hunter of the neighbourhood, to explain, to make, to bind*
ilammi ...	,,		
481*a*. cilidagal ...	𒌋𒌋 𒇉	?	*library*
482. ?	𒈫 𒐀	*	*such an one (so and so)*
483. ip (ib, ibbi)...	𒅁	banu, ligittu, tupuktu	*to create, log* (measure), *race*
dar	,,	nibittu, gisru ...	*name, strong*
daruv ...	,,	izkhu	?
uras... ...	,,	sa-issik-icribi, baru, ramcu, urasu, acmu, ligittu, nibittu	*who hears prayers, ?, a herd, ?, log, name*
484. lu	𒇻, 𒈝	tsini, cirru	*flocks, sheep*
dib (dip) ...	,,	dibbu, lavu, etiku, tsabatu, titsbatu, tamkhu	*tablet, tablet, to cross, to seize, seizure, hold*
udu, dū ...	,,	immiru, dassu ...	*lamb, gazelle*
u, sib (sip) ...	,,		
guccal ...	,,	guccallu	?
	,,	cavu, bahu, garru ...	*to burn* (?), *chaos, food*

Phonetic Value (Accadian word).	Cuneiform Character.	Assyrian rendering.	Meaning.
485. ki, kin (cin)	𒅗, 𒅗, 𒅗	turtu, sipru, pāru, sitehu, senikhu, amaru	*dove*(?), *writing* (explanation), ?, ?, ?, *messenger*
486. sak, sik ...	𒅗	saradu	*paint*
śik, ukh ...	,,	supātu, sipatu ...	*cloth, stuff*
mut (?) ...	,,		
487. ?	𒅗, 𒅗		*plank*
488. sis	𒅗	pasāsu	*to extend* (?)
busus (*Ass. value*)	,,	damamu	*to perish*
489. ?	𒅗	tur-sipri	*librarian* (scribe)
490. dar (dara) ...	𒅗	dahmu	?
491. munsub ...	𒅗	khir-tū	?
492. gur	𒅗	carū	? .
493. erin	𒅗	erinu	*cedar* (?)
494. lig (lik) ...	𒉌	calbu, pultu, baltu, uru	*dog*, ?, ?, *lion*
tas (das) ...	,,	nisu (?), nacaru ...	*man, enemy*
lis	,,		
ur (*Ass. value*)	,,	nesu	*lion*
495. dhu	𒅗	cibu, alacu	*mass* (body, weight), *to go*
al	,,	pāsu, apasu, sundu, rucdu	?, ?, ?, ?, ?
496. śal, rak ...	𒊩, 𒊩	nestu, uru	*a woman, a city*
kal (gal), mu-rub	,,	uru	*a city*
mak, muk ...	,,	muccu	*a building*
496*a*. murub ...	𒊩	uru	*a city*
496*b*. murub ...	𒊩	pū, uśukhu	*mouth*, ?

Phonetic Value (Accadian word).	Cuneiform Character.	Assyrian rendering.	Meaning.
497. gar		nan * *	?
498. nin, ni, mak...		beltu, rubatu ...	*lady; princess*
499. dam (dav) ...		assatu, allatu, [mutu]	*woman, wife, [husband]*
500. gu		kā, īlu-sa-napkhari, mātu, pānu	*?, god of the world, land, face*
501. ?		?	?
502. tsu, tsum, rak, ri, khal (khil)		?	?
503. nik (nig) ...		?	?
504. i		?	?
505. el (il) ... (*See No.* 211)	,,	śikhapcu, ellu, bibu teliltu	*?, high (?), ?* *hymn*
506. lum, khum ...		unnubu	?
507. mun, mur, ucu		labinu, libittu, malgu, Śivannu	*brick, brickwork, brick, the month Sivan*
508. ?		ussusu	*foundation*
509. su, mastenu		baru, eribu, nikhappu, lēmu, śakhpu, asaru, śikhu, caramu, adaru, khīsu, cissatu	*?, to set, ?, ?, overthrow, a place (?), plague, a vineyard (?), darkness (?), ?, multitude*
essā... ...	,,	sepu...	*a foot*
su	,,	mastenu	*mischief*
dhiv, sumasdin	,,	essutu	*change (time)*
510. śik (sik, sig)		siktu, matsu, mātu, ensu, nadkhu, śakhpu	*?, to find (?), country, sick, fragment, overthrow*
510a. ?		?	*" a sixtieth"* (Oppert)

Phonetic Value (Accadian word).	Cuneiform Character.	Assyrian rendering.	Meaning.
511. pis	⟪cuneiform⟫	khumtsiru	?
cis	,,	pešu	?
* mis ...	,,	citstu	jungle
512. ?	⟪cuneiform⟫	pulukhtu ...	fear (worship)
513. gibil ...	⟪cuneiform⟫	kilutu	a burning
cibir ...	,,	sarapu, makiddu ...	to burn, a burning
514. en	⟪cuneiform⟫	siptu	lip (paragraph, incantation)
515. isi, śulsa, sukhul	⟪cuneiform⟫		?,
sukhub ...	,,	śūppatu	
516. sutul, sudun	⟪cuneiform⟫	nīru	yoke
517. ?	⟪cuneiform⟫	isatu...	fire
518. khul ...	⟪cuneiform⟫	khidutu	sin
ucus ...	,,	cissu, padu	multitude, ?
bibra ...	,,	bibru, nigu	joy (?), authority
519. dhul ...	⟪cuneiform⟫	?	?
520. śik	⟪cuneiform⟫	?	?
521. sikka ...	⟪cuneiform⟫	atudu	he-goat
522. ?	⟪cuneiform⟫	?	?

N.B.—A Star (*) signifies that one or more characters have been lost by a fracture of the tablet. *Khi*, a value of No.. 180, has been accidentally omitted.

The following is a list of the characters which express the open or simple syllables of the Assyrian alphabet. The beginner is advised to commit it to memory before advancing further in the study of the language. The letters of the Hebrew alphabet are added in order to explain the transliteration adopted for Assyrian sounds.

א, *a, à, ha* 𒀀

ב, *b.* | *ab*, *ib*, *ub*. | *ba*, *bi*, *bu*, *be.*
ב, *p.* | | *pa*, *pi*, *or pu.*

ג, *g.* | | *ga*, *gi*, *gu*, *ge.*
ד, *c.* | *ag*, *ig*, *ug.* | *ca*, *ci*, *cu.*
ק, *k.* | | *ka*, *ki*, *ku.*

ד, *d.* | | *da*, *di*, *du*, *de.*
ט, *dh.* | *ad*, *id*, *ud.* | *dha*, *or dhi*, *dhu*, *dhe.*
ת, *t.* | | *ta*, *ti*, *tu*, *te.*

ה, *h.*   *ah, hi, h,*   *uh.*

ו, *u, v.*   *hu, ù,*   *u,*   *va, u.*   *See also* m.

ז, *z.* | | *za*, *zi*, *zu.*
ס, *s.* | *az*, *iz*, *uz.* | *śa*, *śi*, *śu.*
צ, *ts.* | | *tsa*, *tsi*, *tsü.*

ח, *kh.*   *akh,*   *ikh and ukh,*   *ukh ;*   *kha,*   *khi,*   *khu.*

י, *i.*   *i, 'i.*

ל, *l.*   *al,*   *il,*   *ul,*   *el ;*   *la,*   *li,*   *or lu.*

▢, *m*, also *v*.   〴 {am, av,}   〴 {im, iv,}   〴 {um; uv;} | 〴 or 〴 {ma, va,}   〴 {mi, vi,}   〴 {nu, vu,}   〴 {me ve}.

𒉌, *n*.   〴 an,   〴 or 〴 in, | 〴 na,   〴 ni,   〴 nu,   〴 ne.   〴 un,   〴 en.

𒅀, *e*.   〴.

𒊑, *r*.   〴 ar,   〴 ir,   〴 or 〴 ur. | 〴 ra,   〴 ri,   〴 or 〴 ru.

𒊭, *s*.   〴 or 〴 as,   〴 is,   〴 us,   〴 es. | 〴 or 〴 sa,   〴 si,   〴 or 〴 su,   〴 or 〴 se.

Diphthongs :—〴 〴 ai (*aya*), 〴 ya (*ia*).

An ideograph is often indicated by a *phonetic complement* which gives the first or last syllable of the Assyrian word which is to be read. Thus 〴 〴 is to be rendered by some part (according to the context) of the aorist *acsud* " I acquired."

Three main rules to be observed in selecting the value of a character are (1) that that power is to be chosen, the first or last consonant of which is the same as the consonant which ends the preceding syllable or begins the next; (2) that no Assyrian word, as a general rule, ought to contain more than three radical letters ; and (3) that values consisting only of a consonant and a vowel are to be preferred to those in which the vowel is enclosed between two consonants.

An open syllable (that is, one which begins with a vowel) only exceptionally follows a character which terminates in a consonant; and all words end with the line. Determinative Prefixes (D.P) are a great assistance to the reader. These are unpronounced ideographs which are always set before certain classes of persons and objects ; so that their presence enables us to tell with certainty the nature of the following word. There are also Determinative Affixes (D.A.) which serve the same purpose.

The determinative prefixes and affixes are as follows :

PREFIXES :—

►►𝈀 (*'ilu*)	denotes	a god or goddess.
𝈀 or 𝈀𝈀𝈀	„	a man.
𝈀-	„	a woman.
►=𝈀𝈀 or ►𝈀 (*âlu*)	„	a city or town.
⋋ (*matu*)	„	a country.
𝈀𝈀 ▱ (*nahru*)	„	a river.
=𝈀𝈀𝈀 or ▱𝈀 (*bîtu*)	„	a house.
⋋𝈀 (*rukhu*)	„	wind, or point of the compass.
⟨▥ (*tulu*)	„	a mound.
▱⋋𝈀 (*abnu*)	„	a stone.
⟨𝈀𝈀 (*illu*)	„	a metal.
▱𝈀 (*etsu*)	„	tree or wood.

PREFIXES :—

►𝈀⋋ (*kanu*)	denotes	grass, reeds, &c.
⋈▥ (*'imiru*)	„	animal.
►𝈀⟨𝈀⋋ ⋋𝈀 (*itstsuru*)	„	a bird.
⋋►𝈀𝈀𝈀	„	an insect.
▱►𝈀	„	an official or class of persons.
►𝈀𝈀 (*bilu*)	„	a ruler.
⋋⋋⋋ (*seru*)	„	a limb or body.
►⋋𝈀 or ⋘⋘𝈀 (*arkhu*)	„	a month.
▥𝈀 (*lubustu*)	„	clothing.
⋈⋈𝈀►►𝈀 (*cacabu*) or ⟨⋈𝈀⋋ }	„	a star.

AFFIXES :—

𝈀⋘	denotes	the plural.
𝈀𝈀	„	the dual.
⋋►⋋	„	an ordinal number.

AFFIXES :—

⟨▥ (*irtsitu*)	denotes	a place.
►𝈀𝈀 (*itstsuru*)	„	a bird.

THE NOUNS.

Nouns substantive and adjective do not differ in form in Assyrian.

The adjective always follows its substantive, and has neither comparative nor superlative.

Nouns are of two genders, masculine and feminine, and abstract nouns take the feminine form. Many words are both masculine and feminine, and may take the terminations of both genders.

There are two numbers, singular and plural; and a dual is found in the case of those nouns which denote doubles, like "the eyes." Adjectives as well as substantives admit the dual form.

There are three cases, the nominative, ending in *-u;* the genitive, ending in *-i;* and the accusative, ending in *-a;* but great laxity prevails in the use of these forms.

The case-terminations have a final *m* (or *v*), termed the *mimmation*. This was usually dropped in the later Assyrian inscriptions, though the Babylonian dialect preserved it to the last.

When one substantive governs another, the governing noun loses the case-endings (and mimmation), and the governed noun which immediately follows commonly assumes the termination of the genitive. Thus *bil* is "lord," but *bil nuri*, "lord of light."

The feminine singular changes the *u* of the nominative masculine into *-ūtu*, *-ătu*, and *-ĭtu* (or *ĕtu*). The last two forms (*ătu* and *ĭtu*) might elide the vowel, unless the root is a "surd" one, like *šar*, when the final letter is doubled, producing *šarrătu*, "queen." In the plural the feminine ending became *-ātu* and *-ītu* or *-ētu*.

The oldest form of the plural masculine was in *-ānu*, which was originally used for both genders. We also find traces of a reduplicated plural, like *mâmi*, "waters," and of a plural in *-ūnu*, like *dilūnu*, "buckets." Another form of the plural masculine was in *-ūtu* (carefully to be distinguished from the feminine singular in *-ūtu*). This is the form of the masculine plural adopted by all adjectives. The most common termination of the masculine plural was in *-e* or *-i*. These plurals are in many cases indistinguishable from the genitive case of the singular. The ending of the dual was *ā*.

There is a curious plural in *-tan*, which combines the feminine and masculine terminations. It expresses a *collection* of anything, e.g., *e-bir-tā-an*, "a ford."

PARADIGMS OF NOUNS.

The Characters to be transliterated by the Student.			The Characters to be added by the Student.	
Masculines :—				
Sing. Nom. ...	 𒈾𒉌𒊒 (na - ci - ru)	an enemy	mu-śa-ru (*Nos.* 23, 116, 22).	an inscription
„ Gen. ...	 𒈾𒉌𒊑	...	mu-śa-ri	...
„ Acc. ...	 𒈾𒉌𒊏	...	mu-śa-ra	...
Plural	 𒈾𒉌𒊑	...	mu-śa-rē *or* mu-śa-ri	...
Sing. Construct. state	 𒈾𒉌�景	...	mu-śar	...
Sing. Nom. ...	𒈾𒄴𒇻 (na - akh '- lu)	a brook	śar-ru (*Nos.* 193, 22)	a king
„ Gen. ...	 𒈾𒄴𒇷	...	śar-ri	...
„ Acc. ...	𒈾𒄴𒆷	...	śar-ra	...
Plural	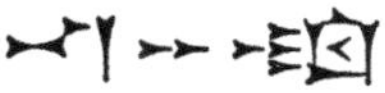 𒈾𒇷	...	śar-ri	...
Sing. Construct. state	 𒈾	...	śar	...
Sing. Nom. ...	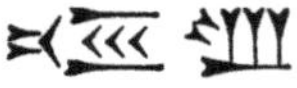 �zic𒊒 (zic - ru)	record	nac-lu (*Nos.* 57, 484)	complete
„ Gen. ...	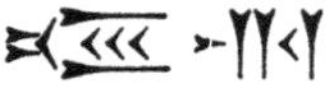 �zic𒊑	...	nac-li	...
„ Acc. ...	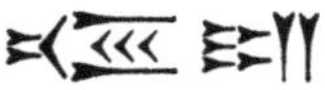 �zic𒊏	...	nac-la	...
Plural Nom. ...	 �zic𒉌𒌓	...	nac-lu-tu	...
„ Gen. ...	 �zic𒉌𒋾	...	nac-lu-ti	...
„ Acc. ...	 �zic𒉌�	...	nac-lu-ta	...

The Characters to be transliterated by the Student.			*The Characters to be added by the Student.*	
Masculines :—				
Construct. Sing.	 𒀭𒁹	*record*	na-cal	*complete*
Construct. Pl....	 𒀭𒁹	...	nac-lu ut...	...
Sing. Nom. ...	 �流	*fortress*	khar-su	*a forest*
„ Gen. ...	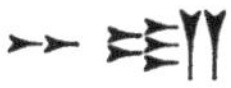 �流	...	khar-si	...
„ Acc. ...	 �流	...	khar-sa	...
Plural Nom. ...	  �流 [*or* �流]	...	khar-sā-nu [*or* khar-sa-a-nu]	...
„ Gen. ...	 �流	...	khar-sā-ni	...
„ Acc. ...	 �流	...	khar-sā-na	...
Construct. Sing.	 𒄲	...	kha-ra-as...	...
Construct. Pl....	 𒄳	...	khar-sā-an	...
Feminines :—				
Sing. Nom. ...	 𒉺	*a lady*	ʼi-lă-tu	*goddess*
„ Gen. ...	 𒉺	...	ʼi-lă-ṭi	...
„ Acc. ...	 𒉺	...	ʼl-lă-ta	...
Plural Nom. ...	 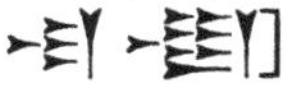 𒉺 [*or* 𒉺]	...	ʼi-lă-a tu [*or* ʼi-lă-tu]	...
„ Gen. ...	  𒉺 [*or* 𒉺]	...	ʼi-la-a-ti [*or* ʼi-la-a-te]	...
„ Acc. ...	 𒉺	...	ʼi-la-a-ta	...

5*

The Characters to be transliterated by the Student.			The Characters to be added by the Student.	
Feminines :—				
Construct. Sing.	𒇻	a lady	'l-lăt...	goddess
Construct. Pl.	𒀭 𒇻 𒈨	...	'i-la-a-at	...
Sing. Nom. ...	𒀭	...	'il-tu	...
„ Gen. ...	𒀭	...	'il-ti...	...
„ Acc. ...	𒀭	...	'il-ta	...
Plural	as before	...	as before	...
Sing. Nom. ...	𒀭 𒇻 𒀭	...	'i-lĭ-tu	...
„ Gen. ...	𒀭 𒇻	...	'i-lĭ-ti	...
„ Acc. ...	𒀭 𒇻	...	'i-lĭ-ta	...
Plural Nom. ...	𒀭 𒇻 𒀭	...	'i-li-e-tu ['ilētu] ...	...
„ Gen. ...	𒀭 𒇻 [or 𒀭]	...	'i-li-e-ti [or 'i-li-e-te]	...
„ Acc. ...	𒀭 𒇻	...	'i-li-e-ta	...
Construct. Sing.	𒇻	...	'i-lĭt	...
Construct. Pl....	𒇻	...	'i-lĭt...	...
Another Plural Noun	𒀭 𒇻	...	'i-li-i-tu	...
	or 𒀭 𒇻	...	or 'i-lĭ-tu	...
	&c., &c.		&c., &c.	

The Characters to be transliterated by the Student.			The Characters to be added by the Student.	
Feminines :—				
Sing. Nom. ...	 𒇷𒌑𒈨	tongue	'um-mu...	mother
„ Gen. ...	 𒇷𒌑𒈨	...	'um-mi	...
„ Acc. ...	 𒇷𒌑𒈨	...	'um-ma...	...
Plural Nom. ...	 𒇷𒌑𒈨𒀀𒌈	...	'um-ma-a-tu ['ummātu]	...
„ Gen. ...	 𒇷𒌑𒈨𒀀𒋾	...	'um-ma-a-ti	...
„ Acc. ...	 𒇷𒌑𒈨𒀀�	...	'um-ma-a-ta	...
Construct. Sing.	 𒇷𒌑𒈨𒀀	...	'um	...
Construct. Pl. ...	 𒇷𒌑𒈨𒀀𒌈	...	'um-ma-a-at	...

Dual :—				
(Nom., Gen., Acc.)	  𒋗𒈨𒈫	the two hands	'uz-na-a ('uznā)	the two ears
	or 𒈨𒈫		se-pa-a (sepa)	the two feet

Nouns to be written in Assyrian characters, and declined :—

		Plural.
cu-du-du (*Nos.* 462, 212, 212)	*carbuncle*	(cu-du-de) (*Nos.* 462, 212, 342)
da-rum-mu (289, 11, 23) ...	*a dwelling*	(da-rum-mi *and* da-rum-me) (289, 11, 374 *or* 434)
ga-ru (227, 22)	*enemy*	(gari *and* ga-ri-e) (227, 83)
di-ku (342, 209)	*soldier*	(di-ku-tu) (342, 209, 60)
ci-su-du (343, 317, 212) ...	*captive*	(ci-su-du-tu) (343, 317, 212, 60)
dan-nu (241, 24)	*strong*	(dan-nu-tu) (241, 24, 60)
dup-pu (174, 321)	*tablet*	(dup-pa-a-nu) (174, 222, 437, 24)
e-mu-ku (239, 23, 209) ...	*deep power*	(e-mu-ka-a-nu) (239, 23, 20, 437, 24)
ri-su	*head*	(ri-sa-a-nu)
ci-sid-tu	*spoils*	(ci-si-da-a-tu)
i-să-tu	*fire*	('i-sa-a-tu)
pul-khă-tu *or* pu-lukh-tu ...	*fear*	(pul-kha-a-tu)
cimmă-tu *or* cim-tu	*family*	(cim-ma-a-tu)
e-li-nĭ-tu	*high*	(e-li-nē-tu)
makh-ri-tu *or* ma-khir-tu ...	*former*	(makh-ra-a-tu)
gar-ru...	*expedition* ...	(gar-rī-tu *or* gar-ri-i-tu)
ag-gul-lu	*wagon*	(ag-gul-la-a-tu)
ap-pa-ru	*a marsh*	(ap-pa-ra-a-te)
ba-bu...	*a gate* ... ... ·	(ba-ba-a-tu)

THE NUMERALS.

The cardinals have two forms, masculine and feminine; but from 3 to 10 the feminine form is used for the masculine, and the masculine form for the feminine.

When the numerals are expressed in symbols Υ signifies "one," $\Upsilon\Upsilon$ "two," and so on. $\langle$ stands for 10, $\langle\Upsilon$ for 11, $\langle\langle$ for 20, &c. $\Upsilon\!\!\succ$ is 100, and $\langle\Upsilon\!\!\succ$ (= 10 × 100) is 1000.

The cardinals are denoted by adding $\triangleleft\!\!\prec$ to the ordinal; thus Υ $\triangleleft\!\!\prec$ is "first."

Sixty was the mathematical unit: the single wedge (Υ) accordingly stands for the *soss*, or *sixty*, as well as for *one*. In fractions it is the understood denominator; thus, $\Upsilon\Upsilon\Upsilon$ $\langle\langle\langle$ (3.30) is 3 $\frac{30}{60}$, *i.e.* $3\frac{1}{2}$.

TABLE OF CARDINAL AND ORDINAL NUMBERS.

			Masculine.	*Feminine.*		
1	=	Υ	a-kha-du, e-du ... es-tin, es-ta-a-nu ...	i-khi-it ... ... ikh-tu	*First* =	makh-ru, ris-ta-a-nu
	(or $\succ$)					
2	=	$\Upsilon\Upsilon$	sa-ni-e, sa-nu-'u, si-nu-'u	sa-ne-tu	*Second* =	san-nu (*fem.* sa-nu-tu)
3	=	$\Upsilon\Upsilon\Upsilon$	sal-sa-tu	sal-su	*Third* =	sal-sa-ai (*fem.* sa-li-is-tu)
4	=	Ψ	ir-bit-tu, ri-ba-a-tu ...	ar-ba-'i, ir-ba'i ...	*Fourth* =	ri-bu
5	=	$\Psi\Upsilon$	kha-mis-tu, kha-mil-tu	kham-sa, kha-an-si ...	*Fifth* =	kha-an-su
6	=	$\Psi\Upsilon\Upsilon$	si-sa-tu	sis-sa, sis-si ...	*Sixth* =	[? sis-su]
7	=		si-bit-tu, si-bi-tu ...	si-ba	*Seventh* =	si-bu-'u, sa-bi-tu
8	=		[sam-na-tu] ...	sam-na	*Eighth* =	[? su-ma-nu]
9	=		[ti-sit-tu]	[ti-is-'a]	*Ninth* =	[ti-su-'u]
10	=	$\langle$	'e-sir-tu, 'es-e-rit, 'es-rit	'es-ru	*Tenth* =	['es-ru]
11	=	$\langle\Upsilon$	[estinesru ?] ...			

15	=	〈𝖜	…	…	…	kha-mis-se-rit
20	=	〈〈	…	…	…	es-ra-'a
30	=	〈〈〈	…	…	…	si-la-sa-'a
40	=	⧼〈〈	…	…	…	ir-ba-'a, ir-ba-ya
50	=	⧼⧼〈	…	…	…	kha-an-sa-'a
60	=	𝗜	…	…	…	sus-su
70	=	𝗜〈	…	…	…	[śi-bu-'a ?]
80	=	𝗜〈〈	…	…	…	?
90	=	𝗜〈〈〈	…	…	…	?
100	=	𝗜⊢	…	…	…	me'
1000	=	〈𝗜⊢	…	…	…	a-la-pu

EXAMPLE : 𝗜𝗜〈𝗜⊢ 𝖜 𝗜⊢ ⧼⧼𝗜 ⊨⊬⊦⟪ = " 2,451 oxen."

In writing "one" we sometimes find the phonetic complement added to the cipher to denote whether it has the masculine or the feminine form. Thus, 𝗜 ⊣𝗜𝗜 (EST-*en*) = *estin*, 𝗜 ⊨⧫𝗜 (IKH-*it*) = *ikhit*.

Fractional numbers are as follows :— ⊨𝗜 ⊨𝗜𝗜𝗜 ⊬ *su-un-nu* (ideographically written ⊬) = "one-half," 𝗜 ⊨⊥𝗜 𝖜 𝗜𝗜 ⊬ *su-us-sa-a-nu* = "one-third," 〈𝗜⊢ ⊨⊥ ⊀⊢ *si-ni-bu* = "two-thirds," ⊱ ⊨⊨𝗜 ⊀⊢ *pa-ra-pu* = "five-sixths," ⧼𝗜𝗜𝗜 ⊀⊢ *ru-bu* = "one-fourth," ⊨⊨𝗜𝗜 ⊨⊳𝗜 *śu-du* = "one-sixth," ⊨⊨𝗜𝗜 ⊨𝗜 ⊬ *śu-ma-nu* = "one-eighth," and 𝗜 ⊨⊥𝗜 𝗜 *su-us-su* = "a sixtieth."

The adverbial numerals were formed by the termination *yānu*, as 𝖜 ⊨⊥ ⊨𝗜𝗜 𝗜𝗜 ⊬ *sa-ni-e-'ā-nu*, or 𝖜 ⊨⊥ ⊨⊨𝗜𝗜 𝗜𝗜 ⊬ *sa-ni-ya-a-nu* "a second time" ("twice"), *sal-si-'a-nu* or *sal-si-ya-a-nu* "a third time." 𝖜 ⊨⊥ ⊣⊨𝗜 *sa-ni-tu* ("repetition") was used for "once," and in the later inscriptions it took the place of the adverbial numerals, e.g., *sa-ni-ti sal-sa* "the third time." *Sal-sa* is expressed in the Behistun inscription by the compound ideograph ⊰⊁.

Among the indefinite numerals may be reckoned ⊳⊔𝗜 ⊨𝗜𝗜 *ca-lu*, ⊳⊔𝗜 ⊣𝗜 *ca-la*, ⊨𝗜𝗜𝗜 *cal*, ⊣〈 ⊀ *cul-lat* "all," ⊰⊁ ⊀⊢ *gab-bu* "all," 〈⊣𝗜𝗜 ⧼𝗜𝗜𝗜 *gim-ru* "the whole," ⊨𝗜 ⊨⊳𝗜 ⊣⊨𝗜 *ma'-du-tu* "much," and ⊳⊔𝗜 ⊨𝗜𝗜𝗜𝗜 ⊣⊨𝗜 *ca-bit-tu* "much."

THE PRONOUNS.

THE PERSONAL PRONOUNS:—

1. *Sing.*	𒅗 𒌍 *or* 𒀭	anacu... ...	= *I*
,, ...	{ yāti ... ... yātima ... }	= *I*
Plural	a-[nakh?]-ni	= *we*
2. *Sing. Masc.*...	atta	= *thou*
,, *Fem.* ...	atti	= *thou*
Com. Gend....	{ cātu ... ... cāta ... ... }	= *thou*
Plural, Masc....	attunu ...	= *you*
,, *Fem.* ...	[at-ti-na] ...	= *you*
3. *Sing. Masc.* ...	{ sū ... ... }	= *he, it, him*
Fem. ...	{ sī ... ... }	= *she, it, her*
Plural, Masc....	{ sūnu ... ... sun ... ... sunūtu ... sunūti ... sunūt ... }	= *they, them*
,, *Fem.* ...	{ sina ... ... sin ... ... sināti ... ... }	= *they, them*

Yā-ti (*yā-ti-ma*) and *cātu* (*cā-ta*) are more substantival in their use than the other forms of the first two personal pronouns, and are generally met with as the first words of a sentence. Besides *yā-ti* we also find 𒂊𒌋 𒀸 *yā-si* and 𒀺 𒀺 𒀸 *ai-si*.

The Possessive Pronouns are suffixed to the Nouns and Verbs. The following is a list of them :—

POSSESSIVE PRONOUN AFFIXES OF THE NOUN.

1. *Sing. Com. Gend.*	𒂊𒌋, 𒀺	ya, ā … … = *my;* also i, as 𒀺 𒐊 to be read 'āb-i, *my father*
Plural ,,	{ 𒌍 / 𒀀 }	ni … … } nu … … } = *our*
2. *Sing. Masc.* …	𒅗	ca, *also* -c … = *thy*
,, *Fem.* …	𒆠	ci … … … = *thy*
Plural, Masc. …	𒆠 𒉡	cunu, *also* cun = *your*
,, *Fem.* …	[𒆠 𒈾]	[cina] … … = *your*
3. *Sing. Masc.* …	𒋗	su, *also* -s … = *his, its*
,, *Fem.* …	{ 𒐊 / 𒀸 }	sa … … … } si … … … } = *her, its*
Plural, Masc. …	𒋗 𒉡	sunu, *also* sun = *their*
,, *Fem.* …	𒀸 𒈾	sina, *also* sin… = *their*

Ya and *ā* were used as the pronoun suffix of the first person if the noun terminated in a vowel, *i* if it terminated in a consonant.

When the noun ends in *d, dh, t, s, s̆, z*, or *ts*, the third person suffix becomes *s̆u, s̆a*, &c., as *khi-ri-it-s̆u* "its ditch," *bit-s̆u* "his house." The last letter of the noun is very frequently assimilated to the *s̆* of the suffix, as *khi-ri-is̆-s̆u, bis̆-su;* and then the reduplication may be dropped, so that we get *khi-ri-s̆u, bi-s̆u*.

In the later period of the language, the possessive pronouns are attached to the substantive *at-tu* "being" or "essence," and the compound is then used as an emphatic repetition of the pronoun; thus ►⟨⊹ ⊑◄⟨⟨ ⊐⊒⟨ ►⊑⊒⟨ ⟨⟨ *zir-ya at-tū-a* = "my own race" (literally "my race (which is) mine "), ⊐⊒⟨ ►⊑⊒⟨ ⟨⟨ ⟨⟨ ⧓⧓► ⊑⟨⟨⟨► ⟨⟨ *at-tu-u-à, a-bu-u-a* "to me (was) my father."

When the accent fell on the last vowel of the noun to which the possessive pronoun was suffixed, the initial consonant of the second and third pronoun suffixes were often doubled, as ⊑⟨⟨⟨⟨ ⧓⧓► ⊐⧓⟨⟨ ⟨ *cir-bu-us-su* "its interior," for *cirbū-su.*

POSSESSIVE PRONOUN SUFFIXES OF THE VERB.

1.	*Sing.*		-anni, -inni, -nni, -ni ...	... *Plural*	-annini, -annu, -nini, -nu	
2.	„	*Masc.*	-acca, -icca, -cca, -ca,·-c	... „	-accunu, -accun, -cunu, -cun	
2.	„	*Fem.*	-acci, -icci, -cci, -ci ...	... „	-accina, -accin, -cina, -cin	
3.	„	*Masc.*	-assu, -issu, -su, -s ...	... „	-assunuti, -assunu, -assun, -sunutu (v), -sunuti (v), -sunuta (v), -sunu, -sun	
3.	„	*Fem.*	-assi, -assa, -ssa, -ssi, -sa, -si ...	„	-assinati, -assina, -assin, -sinatu (v), sinati (v), -sinata (v), -sina, -sin	

A final *n* might be assimilated to the *initial s* of the 3rd person suffix; thus ⊑⊒⟨⟨⟨ ⊑⊒⟨⟨ ►⟨⟨ ⊧ ⊑⟨ ⧓ ►⟨⟨ *in-da-na-as-su-nu-ti* "he gave them," for *inda-nan-sunuti.*

Besides *-cunu*, we also find ⟨⊒⟨ ⧓ ►⟨⟨ *cu-nu-ti*, and besides ⊑⟨ ⧓► ►⟨⟨ *sunuti* and ⟨⟨► ►⟨⟨⟨ ►⟨⟨ *sinati*, we find *su-nu-siv* or *su-nu-si* and *si-na-si-iv*, just as *yāsi* appears by the side of *yāti.*

THE DEMONSTRATIVE PRONOUNS.

	Sing.		Plural.	
Masc. ...	𒀸𒁹𒂊	su'atu, su'ati, su'ata =*this, that* ...	𒀸𒁹𒂊𒋫	su'átunu, su'atun, sâtunu
Fem. ...	𒋝𒁹𒂊	si'atu, ...		
" ...	𒊭𒁹𒂊	sa'atu (*or* sātu), ... sa'ati, sa'ata ...	𒁹𒆠𒋾	su'atina, satina, sinatina
Masc. ...	𒊭𒁹𒁹	sa'asu, *or* sāsu = *this, that*...	𒊭𒁹𒋫	sāsunu, sāsun
Fem. ...	𒊭𒁹𒁹	sa'asa *or* sāsa, sa'asi ... *or* sāsi	𒊭𒁹𒋝𒋾	sa'asina *or* sāsina

Three demonstratives are used to determinate distance, 𒄠 *ammu* or 𒀸 *ma* ("hic") "this by me;" 𒀭 *annu* ("iste") "that by you;" and 𒀊 *'ullu* ("ille") "that by him." Of *ammu* we find only the sing. fem. 𒄠 *ammāte*, and *mā* (𒀸𒁹) or *ma* the contracted form of the sing. masc. *amma*, and the pl. masc. *ammūta*, which is used as a suffix. Thus we have *sar Assur-ma*, "king of this same Assyria;" *anni-ma* or *an-ma*, "myself" (literally, "this person here"); 𒀸𒀭𒋝𒁹𒆠 *ina sanati-ma si'ati* "in this very year." This suffix is especially common at the end of the astrological tablets.

Sing. Masc.... an-nu			*Plural, Masc.*... an-nu-tu, an-nu-tav, an-ni-e	
" " ... an-ni-i, an-ni, a-an-ni			" " ... an-nu-ti	
" " ... an-na-a, an-na				
" *Fem.* ... an-nă-tu, a-a-na-ti			" *Fem.* ... an-na-a-ti, an-nā-tav, an-nī-ti	
" " ... [an-nĭ-tu]			" " ... an-ne-tav, an-ni-tav, an-ni-ti	
" *Masc.*... ul-lu			" *Masc.*... ul-lu-tu	
" " ... ul-li, ul-li-e				
" " ... ul-la				
" *Fem.* ... ul-lă-tu			" *Fem.* ... [ul-la-a-tu]	

From *ullu* was formed in later times the adj. ⟨𒀀𒀀𒀀 𒀀𒀀 𒀀 𒀀 *ulluai* "on the further side."

In the Persian period we find a new demonstrative *'aga*, or *haga*, or *hagat* :

Sing. Masc. ... 𒀀 𒀀𒀀 *'aga, 'a-ga-a, a-ga-h* ... *Com. gen.* ... 𒀀 𒀀𒀀 𒀀 *'a-ga-a*

„ *Fem.* ... 𒀀 𒀀𒀀 𒀀𒀀 *'a-gă-ta*

This pronoun was further compounded with *annu* and the personal pronouns, so as to strengthen the determinative idea ; thus :

Singular, Masc. ... 𒀀 𒀀𒀀 𒀀 𒀀 *'agannu, 'aganna*

„ „ ... 𒀀𒀀𒀀 𒀀 𒀀𒀀 *'aga-su'u, he namely*

Plural, Masc. ... 𒀀 𒀀𒀀 𒀀 𒀀 𒀀 *'agannutu, aganutu*

„ *Fem.* ... 𒀀 𒀀𒀀 𒀀 𒀀 𒀀 *'agannitu, 'aganet*

„ „ ... 𒀀 𒀀𒀀 𒀀 𒀀 *'aga-sunu, they namely*

Instead of *'aga-sū*, *sū-aga* also occurs, and *aga* is frequently used like a mere article.

RELATIVE PRONOUNS.

The Relative Pronoun is ⟐ *sa*, of all numbers and genders, which was originally a demonstrative. It may be understood, as in English, "the man I saw" for "the man *whom* I saw." It is often used to express the periphrastic genitive, when instead of the construct state, the full form of the first noun with the case-ending is given followed by *sa*, which then means exactly our "of." Thus ⟨⟨ ⟐⟐⟐ ⟐ ⅄ ⅄ *sarru sa matâti* "king of the world." Sometimes the first noun was omitted, as *ina sa Garganis* "according to (the maneh) of Carchemish."

The Interrogative Pronoun is ⟨⟨ ⊁ *man-nu*, ⊨⟍ ⊁ *mā-nu*, or ⟨⟨ *man*, "who?" "what," "which." Sometimes it is contracted into *ma-a*. *Mi-e* or *mi* also signified "who," and may be suffixed to *mannu*, forming ⟨⟨ ⊁ ⟍ *mannu-me*, "who."

The Indefinite Pronouns are the indeclinable ⊨⟍ ⊢⟍⊁ ⊨⟍ *ma-nam-ma*, *ma-na-ma*, *man-ma*, *ma-am-man*, *ma-am-ma*, or *ma-num-ma*, "anybody," and ⟨⊨ ⟨⟊ ⊨⟍ *mi-im-ma*, "anything." The negative ⊢⊨⟍ *la* or ⟨⊨⟍⟊ *ul*, joined in the same sentence with these pronouns, gave them a negative meaning, "nobody," "nothing." This negative meaning might be retained even when the accompanying negative was dropped, like *personne*, &c., in French. ⟍⟍ ⟍⟍ ⊫⟍⟍⟍ ⊨⟍ *ai-um-ma* or *ya-um-ma*, with the negative understood, and ⟍⊢⊨⟍ *nin* also, signified "nobody." ⊨⟍ ⊢⟍⟨ ⊨⟍ *matina* was "at any time," or "in any place." The indeclinable ⊨⟍ ⊢⊨⟍ *mala* = "as many as." "Some, others," was expressed by ⟍⟍ ⊁ ⟊⟍ *ā-nu-te—ā-nu-te*, and ⟍⟍ ⟍⟍⟨ ⟨⟍⊨⟍ *a-kha-di—a-kha-di*. *A-kha-ri-tu* = "other," *sa-num-ma* = "another," *estin ana estin* = "one to another."

The Reflexive Pronoun is ⊫⟍⟍ ⊨⟍ ⊁ *ra-ma-nu*, *ra-ma-ni*, *ra-ma-na* "self," to which the possessive pronouns were suffixed, as *ra-ma-ni-ya* "myself," *ra-ma-nu-ca* or *ra-ma-nu-uc-ca* "thyself," *ra-ma-ni-su-un* "themselves." ⊫⟍⟍⟊ ⊫⟍⟍ *gadu* also was used for "individual," and "myself" might be expressed by ⊢⊢⟍ ⊞ ⊨⟍ *an-ni-ma* or ⊢⊢⟍ ⊨⟍ *an-ma* (literally "this (man) here").

THE VERB.

Assyrian Verbs are for the most part triliteral, that is to say, the root consists
f three consonants or semi-consonants.

If the root consist of three consonants the verb is called *complete;* if one
r more of the three radical letters are semi-consonants which easily pass into
owels (*h* or א becoming *a; v* or ו becoming *u; y* or י becoming *i;* and *e* or ע
sing its guttural sound), the verb is called *defective.*

There are four principal Conjugations :—

(1) Kal, the simplest form, with an active (more rarely a neuter) signification, as ⸜𐎗⸜ ⟨𒐊⟩ *ictum* " he concealed."

(2) Niphal, the passive of Kal, formed by prefixing *n*, which may be
assimilated to the following vowel, as ⸜𐎗⸜ ⸜𐎗 ⟨𒐊⟩ *iccatum*
" he was concealed" (for *incatum*).

(3) Pael, with an intensive (and hence, sometimes a causative) signification, formed by doubling the second radical letter of the root,
and conjugating the persons with an inserted *u*, as
⸤𐎗⸤ ⸤𐎗 ⟨𒐊⟩ *yucattum* (=*i-u-cattum*) " he did conceal."

(4) Shaphel, with a causative signification, formed by prefixing *s(a)* to
the root, and conjugating the persons with inserted *u*, as
⸤𐎗⸤ ⸤𐎗⸤ ⟨𒐊⟩ *yusactum* " he caused to conceal."

Instead of Shaphel, concave verbs [*see below*] have *Aphel, s* having been
hanged into *h* and lost, as ⸤𐎗⸤ ⸤𐎗 ⟨𒐊⟩ *yudhib* " he caused to be good."

Each of the four principal conjugations has two secondary forms made by
serting *t* and *tan* after the first consonant; thus :—

(1*a*) Iphteal from Kal, as ⸜𐎗⸜ ⸤𐎗 ⟨𒐊⟩ *ic-ta-tum.*

(1*b*) Iphtaneal from Kal, as ⸜𐎗⸜ ⸤𐎗 ⟨𒐊⟩ *ic-tan-tum.*

(2*a*)   Ittaphal from Niphal, as [cuneiform] *it-ta-ctum* (for *in-ta-ctum*).

(2*b*)   Ittanaphal from Niphal, as [cuneiform] *it-tan-accatum* (for *in-tan-accatum*).

(3*a*)   Iphtaal from Pael, as [cuneiform] *yuc-ta-ttum.*

(3*b*)   Iphtanaal from Pael, as [cuneiform] *yuc-tan-attum.*

(4*a*)   Istaphal from Shaphel, as [cuneiform] *yus-ta-ctum* or *yul-ta-ctum.*

(4*b*)   Istanaphal from Shaphel, as [cuneiform] *yus-tan-actum* or *yul-tan-actum.*

From the Aphel of concave verbs is formed an Itaphal, as [cuneiform] *yu-ta-dhib.*

These secondary conjugations have a reflexive force.

Niphal and Shaphel (and also probably Aphel) admit also of *Paelised* conjugations, (2*c*) Niphael, as [cuneiform] *iccattum,* and (4*c*) Shaphael, as [cuneiform] *yuscattum.*

From Niphal, Pael, and Shaphel, other intensive conjugations could be formed by repeating the last radical : thus (2*nd*) Niphalel, as [cuneiform] *iccatumîm ;* (3*rd*) Palel, as *yucatumîm ;* and (4*th*) Shaphalel, as *yusactumîm.*

Except Kal and Niphal, which stood in the relation of active and passive to one another, the other conjugations had passives formed by changing the vowels of the root into *u,* thus :

(3)   Pael makes [cuneiform] *yucuttum* (permansive, *cuttum*).

(4)   Shaphel makes [cuneiform] *yus-cu-tum* (permansive, *sucutum* or *sucatum*).

Aphel makes [cuneiform] *yudhub.*

(4*a*)   Istaphal makes (permansive) [cuneiform] *sutactim.*

The Moods are five in number—(1) the indicative, (2) the subjunctive, (3) the imperative, (4) the precative, and (5) the infinitive.

The indicative possesses two primary and three secondary TENSES—(1) the permansive or perfect; (2) the aorist or imperfect; (3) the present, a modified form of the aorist; (4) the perfect or pluperfect, the older form of the aorist; and (5) the future, the older form of the present.

The original tenses of the verb were (1) the perfect (permansive) and (2) the imperfect (aorist); but under the influence of Accadian, the imperfect split itself into two forms, one shorter (as 𒌍 𒈨𒐊 *iscun* "he made") and one longer (as 𒂊 𒈨𒐊 *isaccin* "he makes"), which came to be used with a real tense-distinction of meaning (as in Ethiopic). The longer and more primitive form of the present (*isaccinu*) came further to be used with a future force; and the longer and more primitive form of the aorist (*iscunu*), from its being adopted after words like "when" or "who," came to have generally a perfect or pluperfect sense.

The permansive (perfect) has grown out of the close attachment of abbreviated forms of the personal pronouns to nouns and participles into a true tense.

Besides the apocopated or ordinary aorist (*iscun*) and the pluperfect aorist (*iscunu*), there exists (1) a conditional or motive aorist (*iscuna*) formed by the attachment of *a*, "the augment of motion," to the apocopated aorist, and (2) the energic aorist formed by the retention of the original mimmation, *iscunum(ma)*, *iscunim(ma)*, *iscunam(ma)*. There was also another form of the aorist which ended in *-i* (as *iscuni*).

These terminations of the aorist in *-u, -i, -a*, answer to the three case-endings of the noun, the apocopated aorist corresponding with the construct state, and go back to a time when but little distinction was made between the noun and the verb. The subjunctive mood is used in relative and conditional clauses, and is denoted by the addition of the particle *ni*, which may be placed after the possessive pronoun suffix, as 𒀭 𒂊 𒌋 𒀀 𒂊 𒌍 *ci ikabu-su-ni* "when he had called it."

The imperative is confined to the 2nd person, the 2nd pers. sing. masc. giving the simplest form of the verb (as *sucun, rikhits, tsabat*), the vowels always being the same in both syllables, the 2nd pers. fem. ending in *i* (as *sucini* or *sucni*), the 2nd pers. pl. masc. in *-u* (as *sucinu* or *sucnu*) and the 2nd pers. pl. fem. in *ā* (as *sucinā* or *sucnā*). The 2nd pers. sing. masc. may take the augment of motion *-ă* (as *sucună* or *sucnă*). The precative is formed by prefixing *lu* or *li* (the vowel of which coalesces with the vowel of the person-prefix in the 1st and 3rd persons) to any one of the forms of the aorist. It is generally used in the 3rd person, as *liscun* "may he place." The infinitive is really a verbal substantive and declined accordingly.

Besides the moods, every conjugation possesses a participle, which, except in Kal and the Pael of concave verbs, prefixes *mu-*.

There are three *numbers*, singular, plural, and dual, but the dual which ends in *-ā* is only found in the 3rd person.

There are three Persons in the singular and plural, the 2nd and 3rd having different forms for masculine and feminine.

A feminine nominative, however, is often used improperly with a masculine verb (as ⊢⊣𝕐 ⟨𝕎 ⊨𝕐𝕐𝕐⊨ ⫢⊢⊨𝕀 ⊣𝕐𝕐⟨𝕐 *Istar yusapri* "the goddess Istar disclosed") and on the other hand, in the 2nd pers. plural (especially in the imperative) we frequently find the feminine instead of the masculine form.

There are many contracted forms in the Assyrian verb, produced chiefly by dropping a short *-ĭ* or *-ă;* thus 𝕁𝕀⊢𝕐 ⊨𝕐⊢ ⟨⊨⊨ *tastalmi* for *tastalami*, ⊨ ⊁⟠ ⟨𝕀⧣ *taptikdi* for *taptikidi, ittalcu* for *ittallicu, tasalmu* for *tasallimu, usziz* or *ulziz* for *usaziz.*

D, ts, z, or *s* assimilate the inserted *t* of the secondary conjugations, as ⊨𝕐 𝕐𝕐 ⊣ *its-tsa-bat* for ⊨𝕐 ⊨⊨𝕐𝕐𝕐 ⊣ *its-ta-bat*, ⊨𝕐 𝕐𝕐 ⨯𝕐𝕐𝕐 *iz-za-car* for *iz-ta-car.*

S may change the *t* into *š* becoming *š* itself, as ⊨𝕐 ⧻ ⊨⊨ *iš-ša-can* and *i-ša-can* for ⊨𝕐𝕐 ⊨⊨𝕐𝕐 ⊨⊨ *is-ta-can.*

The enclitic conjunction *vă* ("and)" is attached very closely to the termination of the verb.

PARADIGMS.

The Strong or Complete Verb.

KAL.

The second vowel of the aorist may be either *a*, *i*, or *u*, as *iscun* "he placed," *ipdhir* "he freed," *itsbat* "he took," but *u* is most common.

The third vowel of the present may similarly be either *a*, *i*, or *u*, as *inaccar* "he estranges," *isaccin* "he places," *idammum* "it passes away," but *i* is, by far, the most common vowel.

The first person singular of the aorist sometimes has *e* in Babylonian instead of *a*, as ⟨⟨⟨ 𒀀𒈾 *esnik* for *asnik*, and verbs א״פ (see *infra*) in Assyrian might adopt the same vowel.

PERMANSIVE [*or* Perfect].—*Singular.*				PRESENT.—*Singular.*		
I.	𒊍𒈾 𒀉 𒅗		sac-na-cu *or* sac-na-ac	𒀀𒊍𒈾 𒂟		a-sac-cin "*I place*"
2. *Masc.*	,,	,,	sac-na at	,,	,,	ta-sac-sin
2. *Fem.*	,,	,,	[? sac-na-ti]	,,	,,	ta-sac-ci-ni
3. *Masc.*	,,	,,	sa-cin (𒊍 𒂟)	,,	,,	i-sac-cin
3. *Fem.*	,,	,,	sac-nat	,,	,,	ta-sac-cin
		Plural.			*Plural.*	
I.	,,	,,	?	𒉌𒊍𒈾 𒂟		ni-sac-cin
2. *Masc.*	,,	,,	?	,,	,,	ta-sac-ci-nu
2. *Fem.*	,,	,,	?	,,	,,	ta-sac-ci-na
3. *Masc.*	,,	,,	sac-nu	,,	,,	i-sac-ci-nu
3. *Fem.*	,,	,,	sac-na	,,	,,	i-sac-ci-na
		Dual.			*Dual.*	
3.	𒊍𒈾 𒀉 𒈦		sac-na-a [sacnā]	,,	,,	[i-sac-ci-na-a]

AORIST.

Singular.

1.	𒀸 as-cun ("*I placed*");		ar-khi-its ("*I inundated*");		ats-bat ("*I took*")
2. *Masc.*	„ „ tas-cun;	„ „	tar-khi-its;	„ „	ta-ats-bat
2. *Fem.*	„ „ tas-cu-ni;	„ „	tar-khi-tsi;	„ „	ta-ats ba-ti
3. *Masc.*	„ „ is-cun;	„ „	ir-khi-its;	„ „	its-bat
3. *Fem.*	„ „ tas-cun;	„ „	tar-khi-its;	„ „	ta-ats-bat

Plural.

1.	ni-is-cun;		ni-ir-khi-its;		ni-its-bat
2. *Masc.*	„ „ tas-cu-nu;	„ „	tar-khi-tsu;	„ „	ta-ats-ba-tu
2. *Fem.*	„ „ tas-cu-na;	„ „	tar-khi-tsa;	„ „	ta-ats-ba-ta
3. *Masc.*	„ „ is-cu-nu;	„ „	ir-khi-tsu;	„ „	its-ba-tu
3. *Fem.*	„ „ is-cu-na;	„ „	ir-khi-tsa;	„ „	its-ba-ta

Dual.

3.	{is-cu-na-a [ⁱiscunā]; }	ir-khi-tsa-a;	its-ba-ta-a

The student will form the future and pluperfect by attaching the vowel -*u* to those singular forms of the present and aorist which end in a consonant, and -*uni* (also -*unu*, -*unuv*, and -*univ*) to those plural forms of the same tenses which end in a consonant.

IMPERATIVE.

Sing. 2. *Masc.*	su-cun;		ri-khi-its;		tsa-bat
„ 2. *Fem.*	„ „ su-ci-ni *or* su-uc-ni;	„ „	ri-khi-tsi *or* ri-ikh-tsi;	„	tsa-ba-ti *or* tsa-ab-ti
Plu. 2. *Masc.*	„ „ su-ci-nu *or* su-uc-nu;	„ „	ri-khi-tsu *or* ri-ikh-tsu;	„	tsa-ba-tu *or* tsa-ab-tu
„ 2. *Fem.*	„ „ su-ci-na *or* su-uc-na;	„ „	ri-khi-tsa *or* ri-ikh-tsa;	„	tsa-ba-ta *or* tsa-ab-ta

PRECATIVE.

Singular.

.	𒐀		lu-us-cun;			lu-ur-khi-its;		lu-uts-bat
. *Masc.*	,,	,,	lu-tas-cun ;	,,	,,	lu-tar-khi-its ;	.,	., lu-ta-ats-bat
. *M. & F.*	,,	,,	li-is-cun ;	,,	,,	li-ir-khi-its ;	,,	,, li-its-bat

Plural.

. *Masc.*		li-is-cu-nu ;	li-ir-khi-tsu ;
. *Fem.*	,,	,, li-is-cu-na ;	,, ,, li-ir-khi-tsa ;
. *Masc.*		li-its-ba-tu	
. *Fem.*	,,	,, li-its-ba-ta	

The augment of motion and the mimmation may be attached to all the above forms. When the augment of motion is attached to the 2nd person masc. plur. of the imperative *u*+*a* passes through *va* into *ā ;* thus 𒐀 *u-uc-nā* (or 𒐀 *su-uc-na-a*) instead of *su-uc-nu-a*.

INFINITIVE.				PARTICIPLE.		
	sā-cā-nu	*to dwell.*			sā-ci-nu	*dwelling.*
	ra-kha-tsu	*to inundate.*			rā-khi-tsu	*inundating.*
	tsa-ba-tu	*to seize.*			tsā-bi-tu	*seizing.*

IPHTEAL.

PERMANSIVE (Perfect).			PRESENT.	
Singular.			*Singular.*	
1.	𒑄𒐚𒑊𒐚 sit-cu-na-cu ...		𒑊𒑊𒑊 as-tac-can	
			𒑊𒑊𒑊 as-ta-can	
			𒑊𒑊𒑊 al-ta-can	
2. *Masc.*	„ „ [sit-cu-na-at] ...		„ „ tas-tac-can, *&c.*	
2. *Fem.*	„ „ ?		„ „ tas-tac-ca-ni	
3. *Masc.*	„ „ sit-cun ...		„ „ is-tac-can	
3. *Fem.*	„ „ sit-cu-nat ...		„ „ tas-tac-can	
Plural.			*Plural.*	
1.	„ „ ?		𒑊𒑊𒑊 nis-tac-can	
2. *Masc.*	„ „ ?		„ „ tas-tac-ca-nu	
2. *Fem.*	„ „ ?		„ „ tas-tac-ca-na	
3. *Masc.*	„ „ sit-cu-nu ...		„ „ is-tac-ca-nu	
3. *Fem.*	„ „ sit-cu-na ...		„ „ is-tac-ca-na	
Dual.			*Dual.*	
3.	„ „ [sit-cu-na-a] ...		[is-tac-ca-na-a]	

AORIST.
Singular.

1.	𒑊𒑊𒑊 as-ta-cin, al-ta-cin ;		𒑊𒑊𒑊 ap-te-kid *"I overlooked"*	
2. *Masc.*	„ „ tas-ta-cin, *&c.;*		„ „ ta-ap-te-kid	
3. *Fem.*	„ „ tas-ta-ci-ni ;		„ „ ta-ap-te-ki-di	
3. *Masc.*	„ „ is-ta-cin ;		„ „ ip-te-kid	
3. *Fem.*	„ „ tas-ta-cin ;		„ „ ta-ap-te-kid	

Plural.

1.	𒑊𒑊𒑊 nis-ta-cin ;		𒑊𒑊𒑊 ni-ip-te-kid	
2. *Masc.*	„ „ tas-ta-ci-nu ;		„ „ ta-ap-te-ki-du	
2. *Fem.*	„ „ tas-ta-ci-na ;		„ „ tap-te-ki-da	
3. *Masc.*	„ „ is-ta-ci-nu ;		„ „ ip-te-ki-du	
3. *Fem.*	„ „ is-ta-ci-na ;		„ „ ip-te-ki-da	

Dual.

3.	„ „ [is-ta-ci-na-a]		„ „ [ip-te-ki-da-a]	

IPHTEAL—*continued.*

IMPERATIVE.

	Singular.		Plural.	
2. *Masc.*	𒅆𒄿𒅆	sit-cin	𒅆𒄿𒅆	sit-ci-nu
2. *Fem.*	,, ,,	sit-ci-ni	,, ,,	sit-ci-na

PRECATIVE.
Singular.

1.	𒅆𒄿𒅆𒄿	lu-us-ta-can ;	𒅆𒄿𒅆	lu-up-te-kdi
3.	,, ,,	li-is-ta-can ;	,, ,,	li-ip-te-kid

Plural.

3. *M.*	𒅆𒄿𒅆𒄿	li-is-ta-ca-nu ;	𒅆𒄿𒅆	li-ip-te-ki-du
3. *F.*	,, ,,	li-is-ta-ca-na ;	,, ,,	li-ip-te-ki-da

INFINITIVE.

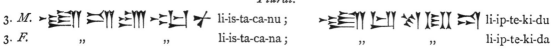 sit-cu-nu ;   pit-ku-du

PARTICIPLE.

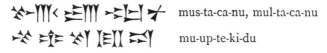 mus-ta-ca-nu, mul-ta-ca-nu

mu-up-te-ki-du

NIPHAL.

PERMANSIVE (Perfect).		PRESENT.

PERMANSIVE (Perfect).

Singular.

1. ... ... [na-as-cu-na-cu]
2. *Masc.* ... ... [na-as-cu-na-at]
2. *Fem.* ... ... ?
3. *Masc.* na-as-cun
3. *Fem.* „ „ [na-as-cu-nat]

Plural.

1. ? „ „ ... ...
2. *Masc.* ? „ „ ... ...
2. *Fem.* ? „ „ ... ...
3. *Masc.* na-as-cu-nu
3. *Fem.* „ „ na-as-cu-na

Dual.

3. ... ... [na-as-cu-na-a]

PRESENT.

Singular.

as-sa-can
„ „ tas-sa-can
„ „ tas-sa-ca-ni
„ „ is-sa-ca-an
„ „ tas-sa-can

Plural.

ni-is-sa-can
„ „ tas-sa-ca-nu
„ „ tas-sa-ca-na
is-sa-ca-nu
„ „ is-sa-ca-na

Dual.

„ „ [is-sa-ca-na-a]

IMPERATIVE.

Singular.

2. *Masc.* na-as-cin
2. *Fem.* „ „ na-as-ci-ni

Plural.

2. *Masc.* „ „ na-as-ci-nu
2. *Fem.* „ „ na-as-ci-na

PRECATIVE.

Singular.

1. lu-us-sa-cin
3. „ „ li-is-sa-cin

Plural.

3. *Masc.* „ „ lis-sa-ci-nu, lis-sac-nu
3. *Fem.* „ „ lis-sa-ci-na, lis-sac-na

AORIST.

Singular.

1. as-sa-cin, as-sa-cun
2. *Masc.* „ „ tas-sa-cin, tas-sa-cun
2. *Fem.* „ „ tas-sa-ci-ni, tas-sa-cu-ni
3. *Masc.* „ „ is-sa-cin, is-sa-cun
3. *Fem.* „ „ tas-sa-cin, tas-sa-cun

AORIST—*Continued.*

Plural.

1.	𒀭𒉺𒊭𒋆		na-as-sa-cin, na-as-sa-cun
2. *Masc.*	,,	,,	tas-sa-ci-nu, tas-sa-cu-nu
2. *Fem.*	,,	,,	tas-sa-ci-na, tas-sa-cu-na
3. *Masc.*	,,	,,	is-sa-ci-nu, is-sa-cu-nŭ
3. *Fem.*	,,	,,	is-sa-ci-na, is-sa-cu-na

Dual.

3.	,,	,,	[is-sa-ci-na-a]

INFINITIVE.

na-as-ca-a-nu [nascānu]

PARTICIPLE.

mu-se-es-sa-ci-nu [musessacinu]

ISTAPHAL.

PERMANSIVE (*or* Perfect).	PRESENT.
Singular.	*Singular.*
1. [na-as-te-cu-na-cu?], &c.	1. 𒀭𒈨𒉆𒊏 at-ta-as-can, &c.
IMPERATIVE.	PRECATIVE.
Singular.	*Singular.*
2. *Masc.* ni-tas-cin (?), &c.	3. „ „ li-it-tas-cin, &c.

AORIST.	INFINITIVE.	PARTICIPLE.
Singular.	na-at-sa-cā-nu	mut-tas-ca-nu
1. 𒀭𒈨𒉆𒊏 at-ta-as-cin at-ta-as-cun, &c.		

PAEL.

PERMANSIVE (*or* Perfect).			PRESENT.		
Singular.			*Singular.*		
1.	𒊹𒈨𒉆𒉌𒈨	sac-ca-na-cu	1.	𒈨𒊹𒊏	u-sac-can
2. *Masc.*	„ „	[sac-ca-na-at]	2. *Masc.*	„ „	tu-sac-can
2. *Fem.*	„ „	?	2. *Fem.*	„ „	tu-sac-ca-ni, tu-sac-ni
3. *Masc.*	𒊹𒊏	sac-can	3. *Masc.*	„ „	yu-sac-can
3. *Fem.*	„	sac-ca-nat	3. *Fem.*	„ „	tu-sac-can
Plural.			*Plural.*		
1.	...	?	1.	𒉡𒊹𒊏	nu-sac-can
2. *Masc.*	...	?	2. *Masc.*	„ „	tu-sac-ca-nu
2. *Fem.*	...	?	2. *Fem.*	„ „	tu-sac-ca-na
3. *Masc.*	...	sac-ca-nu	3. *Masc.*	„ „	yu-sac-ca-nu
3. *Fem*	...	[sac-ca-na]	3. *Fem.*	„ „	yu-sac-ca-na
Dual.			*Dual.*		
3.	...	[sac-ca-na-a]	3.	„ „	[yu-sac-ca-na-a]

PAEL—*continued.*

IMPERATIVE.

Singular.

2. *Masc.*		suc-cin (su-cin)
2. *Fem.*	”	suc-ci-ni

Plural.

2. *Masc.*		suc-ci-nu
2. *Fem.*	”	suc-ci-na

PRECATIVE.

Singular.

1.		lu-sac-can
3.	” ”	lu-sac-can, lu-sac-cin

Plural.

3. *Masc.*		lu-sac-ca-nu
3. *Fem.*	” ”	lu-sac-ca-na

AORIST.

Singular.

1.		u-sac-cin u-sac-cun u-sic-cin
2. *Masc.*	” ”	tu-sac-cin tu-sac-cun tu-sic-sin
2. *Fem.*	” ”	tu-sac-si-ni, &c.
3. *Masc.*	” ”	yu-sac-cin
3. *Fem.*	” ”	tu-sac-cin

Plural.

1.		nu-sac-cin
2. *Masc.*	” ”	tu-sac-ci-nu
2. *Fem.*	” ”	tu-sac-ci-na
3. *Masc.*	” ”	yu-sac-ci-nu
3. *Fem.*	” ”	yu-sac-ci-na

Dual.

3.	” ”	[yu-sac-ci-na-a]

INFINITIVE.

 sac-cā-nu [*but the infin. passive is more common*]

Infin. pass. suc-cu-nu

PARTICIPLE.

 mu-sac-ci-nu

---

From its intensive signification Pael comes sometimes to be used in a causative sense. When Kal is intransitive, Pael is transitive.

N.B.—The present and aorist of Pael are distinguished from the present of Kal by the vowel *u* in the first syllable.

The reduplication is often neglected in writing. It is sometimes replaced in the case of labials and dentals by *mb* (*mp*) and *nd* (*ndh*, *nt*).

IPHTAEL.

PERMANSIVE. *Not found.*

PRESENT.

	Singular.				Plural.	
1.	𒌋𒋻𒃶		us-tac-can	𒀸 𒌋𒋻𒃶		nu-us-tac-can
2. *Masc.*	,,	,,	tu-us-tac-can	,,	,,	tu-us-tac-ca-nu
2. *Fem.*	,,	,,	tu-us-tac-ca-ni	,,	,,	tu-us-tac-ca-na
3. *Masc.*	,,	,,	yus-tac-can	𒌋𒋻𒃶𒃵𒀸		yus-tac-ca-nu
3. *Fem.*	,,	,,	tu-us-tac-can	,,	,,	yus-tac-ca-na

Dual.

	,,	,,	[yus-tac-ca-na-a]

AORIST.

Singular.

1.	𒌋𒋻𒆗		us-tac-cin ;	𒌁𒋆𒐼		up-te-kid	
2. *Masc.*	,,	,,	tu-us-tac-cin ;	,,	,,	tu-up-te-kid
2. *Fem.*	,,	,,	tu-us-tac-cin ;	,,	,,	tu-up-te-ki-di
3. *Masc.*	,,	,,	yus-tac-cin ;	,,	,,	yup-te-kid
3. *Fem.*	,,	,,	tu-us-tac-cin ;	,,	,,	tu-up-te-kid

Plural.

1.	𒀸𒌋𒋻𒆗		nu-us-tac-cin ;	𒀸𒌁𒋆𒐼		nu-up-te-kid	
2. *Masc.*	,,	,,	tu-us-tac-ci-nu ;	,,	,,	tu-up-te-ki-du
2. *Fem.*	,,	,,	tu-us-tac-ci-na ;	,,	,,	tu-up-te-ki-da
3. *Masc.*	𒌋𒋻𒃵𒀸		yus-tac-ci-nu ;	𒋆𒐼𒃵𒃶		yup-te-ki-du
3. *Fem.*	,,	,,	yus-tac-ci-na ;	,,	,,	yup-te-ki-da

Dual.

3.	,,	,,	[yus-tac-ci-na-a]

IPHTAEL—*continued*.

IMPERATIVE. *Not found.*

PRECATIVE.

Singular.		Plural.	
3. 𒁹𒁹𒁹𒁹 lu-us-tac-can	3. *Masc.* 𒁹𒁹𒁹𒁹𒁹	lu-us-tac-**ca-nu**	
	3. *Fem.* ,, ,,	lu-us-tac-**ca-na**	

INFINITIVE.	PARTICIPLE.
[sa-tac-cā-nu]	𒁹𒁹𒁹𒁹 mus-tac-ci-nu

SHAPHEL.

PERMANSIVE. *Not found.*

PRESENT.		AORIST.	
Singular.		*Singular.*	
1. [cuneiform]	u-sa-as-can	1. [cuneiform]	u-sa-as-cin, u-se-es-cin
2. *Masc.* [cuneiform]	tu-sa-as-can	2. *Masc.* ,, ,,	tu-sa-as-cin, &c.
2. *Fem.* ,, ,,	tu-sa-as-ca-ni	2. *Fem.* ,, ,,	tu-sa-as-ci-ni
3. *Masc.* ,, ,,	yu-sa-as-can	3. *Masc.* ,, ,,	yu-sa-as-cin
3. *Fem.* ,, ,,	tu-sa-as-can	3. *Fem.* ,, ,,	tu-sa-as-cin
Plural.		*Plural.*	
1. [cuneiform]	nu-sa-as-can	1. [cuneiform]	nu-sa-as-cin
2. *Masc.* ,, ,,	tu-sa-as-ca-nu	2. *Masc.* ,, ,,	tu-sa-as-ci-nu
2. *Fem.* ,, ,,	tu-sa-as-ca-na	2. *Fem.* ,, ,,	tu-sa-as-ci-na
3. *M.* [cuneiform]	yu-sa-as-ca-nu	3. *Masc.* ,, ,,	yu-sa-as-ci-nu
3. *Fem.* ,, ,,	yu-sa-as-ca-na	3. *Fem.* ,, ,,	yu-sa-as-ci-na
Dual.		*Dual.*	
3.	[yu-sa-as-ca-na-a]	3.	[yu-sa-as-ci-na-a]

IMPERATIVE.		PRECATIVE.	
Singular.		*Singular.*	
2. *Masc.* [cuneiform]	su-us-cin	1.	lu-sa-as-cin
2. *Fem.* ,, ,,	su-us-ci-ni	3.	lu-sa-as-can
Plural.		*Plural.*	
2. *Masc.* ,, ,,	su-us-ci-nu	3. *M.* [cuneiform]	lu-sa-as-ci-nu
2. *Fem.* ,, ,,	su-us-ci-na	3. *Fem.* ,, ,,	lu-sa-as-ci-na

INFINITIVE.

[cuneiform] sa-as-cā-nu [*but the Infin. passive*   [cuneiform] su-us-cu-nu
is more common].

PARTICIPLE.

[cuneiform] mu-sa-as-ci-nu

ISTAPHAL.

PERMANSIVE. *Not found.*

PRESENT. *Singular.*		AORIST. *Singular.*	
1. 𒀹 𒁁 𒁹 us-tas-can *or*		1. us-tas-cin *or*	
𒀹 𒁁 𒁹 ul-tas-can, &c.		ul-tas-cin 𒀹 𒁁 𒁹, {us / ul}-te-sib, &c.	

IMPERATIVE. *Singular.*		PRECATIVE. *Singular.*	
2. *Masc.* 𒁹 𒁹 𒁹 𒁹 su-ti-is-cin, &c.		3. 𒁹 𒁹 𒁹 𒁹 lu-us-tas-can, &c.	

INFINITIVE PASSIVE.

𒁹 𒁹 𒁹 𒁹 𒁹 su-te-es-cu-nu.

PARTICIPLE.

𒁹 𒁹 𒁹 𒁹 mus-tas-ci-nu ;   𒁹 𒁹 𒁹 𒁹 mul-tas-ci-nu.

THE WEAK OR DEFECTIVE VERBS.

If one of the radicals of a verb is *n*, *á*, *h*, *u* (*v*), *i* (*y*) or *e*, it differs in many particulars from the conjugation of the Strong Verb, owing to the assimilation of these letters to other vowels or consonants.

Verbs which begin with these letters are called verbs פ״ו, פ״ה, פ״א, פ״ן, פ״י, and פ״ע; verbs which end with them are called verbs ל״ן, ל״א, ל״ה, ל״ו, ל״י, and ל״ע; verbs which have one of these letters as a second radical are called verbs ע״ן, ע״א, ע״ה, ע״ו, ע״י, and ע״ע. The last class of verbs are also called Concave Verbs.

Verbs פ״ן.

N is assimilated to the following letter; though in some few instances we find it irregularly retained. Before *b* or *p* it may be changed to *m*.

	PERMANSIVE.		PRESENT.	
Kal	𒄑𒐕𒌍	na·mir, "*he sees*"	𒂊 𒌋𒐊𒀯 𒌍	i-nam-mir *or* i-nam-mar
Iphteal	𒌍 𒐊𒀭 𒀸𒌍	ni-it-mur	,, ,,	it-ta-mar
Niphal	𒐊𒀯 𒀸𒌍	nam-mur	,, ,,	in-na-mar
Ittaphal	,, ,,	[na-at-te-mur]	𒐊𒀭 𒀸𒐕 𒂊𒐖	it-tam-mar
Pael	𒐊𒀯 𒂊𒐖	nam-mar	,, ,,	yu-nam-mar
Iphtaal	,, ,,	...	𒀸𒐕 𒀸𒐕 𒂊𒐖	yut-tam-mar
Shaphel	,, ,,	[sam-mar]	,, ,,	yu-sam-mar
Istaphal	,, ,,	[sat-ne-mar]	,, ,,	yus-tam-mar
Shaphael	,, ,,	[sa-nam-mar]	,, ,,	yus-nam-mar
Istaphael	,, ,,	...	,, ,,	yus-te-nam-mar
	PASSIVE.		PASSIVE.	
Pael	𒀹𒌍	num-mur	,, ,,	yu-num-mar
Iphtaal	,, ,,	...	,, ,,	yut-tum-mar
Shaphel	{𒌍𒌋𒌍 / 𒌍𒄷𒌍}	su-nu-mur / su-na-mur }	,, ,,	yu-sa-nu-mar
Istaphal	𒌍𒅅𒌋𒌍	su-te-nu-mur	,, ,,	yus-tum-mar
Shaphael	{𒌍𒀹𒌍 / 𒌍𒐊𒀯𒌍}	su-num-mur / su-nam-mur	,, ,,	yus-num-mar

AORIST.

Kal	...	[cuneiform]	im-mur	" *he saw* "
,,	...	[cuneiform]	id-din	" *he gave* "
,,	...	[cuneiform]	ip-pal	" *he threw down* "
,,	...	[cuneiform]	e-cil	" *he ate* "
Iphteal	...	[cuneiform]	it-ta-mir	
Niphal	...	[cuneiform]	in-na-mir	
Ittaphal	...	,, ,,	it-tam-mir	
Pael	...	,, ,,	yu-nam-mir	
Iphtaal	...	,, ,,	yut-tam-mir	
Shaphel	...	,, ,,	yu-sam-mir	
Istaphal	...	,, ,,	yus-tam-mir	
Shaphael	...	,, ,,	yus-nam-mir	
Istaphael	...	,, ,,	yus-te-nam-mir	

IMPERATIVE.

[cuneiform]	u-mur *or* a-mur
[cuneiform]	i-din.
,,	a-pal.
,,	e-cil
,,	ni-it-mir
,,	nam-mir
,,	[ni-tam-mir]
,,	nu-um-mir
	—
,,	su-um-mir
,,	su-ut-tim-mir
,,	su-num-mir
	—

PASSIVE.

Pael	...	[cuneiform]	yu-num-mir
Iphtaal	...	,, ,,	yut-tum-mur
Shaphel	...	,, ,,	ʃyu-sa-nu-mur / yus-nu-mur
Istaphal	...	,, ,,	yus-tum-mur
Shaphael	...	,, ,,	yus-num-mur

PASSIVE.

—
—
—
—
—

PARTICIPLE.

Kal	...	[cuneiform]	nā-mi-ru, nam-ru
Iphteal	...	[cuneiform]	mut-ta-mi-ru
Niphal	...	[cuneiform]	mu-un-nam-mi-ru, mun-nam-ru
Ittaphal	...	[cuneiform]	mut-ta-ma-ru
Pael	...	[cuneiform]	mu-nam-mi-ru
Iphtaal	...	[cuneiform]	mut-tam-mi-ru
Shaphel	...	[cuneiform]	mu-sam-mi-ru
Istaphal	...	[cuneiform]	mus-tam-mi-ru
Shaphael	...	[cuneiform]	mus-nam-mi-ru
Istaphael	...	[cuneiform]	mus-te-nam-mi-ru

Verbs א"פ.

KAL.

PERMANSIVE.		PRESENT.		AORIST.	
Sing. 1.	[asabacu]	𒀀𒋃𒁀𒀊 a-sab "*I sit*"	𒀀𒋃 a-sib, 𒂊𒋃 e-sib
„ 2. *Masc.* ...	[asabat]	„	ta-sab	„	ta-sib
„ 2. *Fem.* ...	—	„	ta-sa-bi	„	ta-si-bi
„ 3. *Masc.* ...	[a-sab]	„	ya-sab, i-sab	„	ya-sib, i-sib 𒂊𒋃
„ 3. *Fem.* ...	—	„	ta-sab	„	ta-sib
Plur. ...	—	𒈾𒋃𒁀𒀊 na-sab	𒈾𒋃 na-sib
„ 2. *Masc.* ...	—	„	ta-sa-bu	„	ta-si-bu
„ 2. *Fem.* ...	—	„	ta-sa-ba	„	ta-si-ba
„ 3. *Masc.* ...	a-sa-bu	„	ya-sa-bu, i-sa-bu	„	ya-si-bu, i-si-bu
„ 3. *Fem.* ...	[a-sa-ba]	„	ya-sa-ba, i-sa-ba	„	ya-si-ba, i-si-ba
Dual, 3. ...	[asabā]	„	[ya-sa-bā]	„	ya-si-bā]

IMPERATIVE AND PRECATIVE.

Sing. 1.	𒇺𒋾𒁍 li-su-ub,	𒇻𒋃 lu-sib
„ 2. *Masc.* ...	„ „	e-sib, a-cul
„ 2. *Fem.* ...	„ „	e-si-bi, a-cu-li
„ 3. *Masc.* ...	„ „	li-su-ub, lu-sib
„ 3. *Fem.* ...	„ „	--
Plur. 1. ...	„ „	—
„ 2. *Masc.* ...	𒂊𒋾𒁍 e-si-bu,	𒀀𒋾𒆷 a-cu-la
„ 2. *Fem.* ...	„ „	e-si-bu, a-cu-la
„ 3. *Masc.* ...	„ „	li-su-bu, lu-si-bu
„ 3. *Fem.* ...	„ „	li-su-ba, lu-si-ba

INFINITIVE.				PARTICIPLE.		
𒊓𒀀𒁍 sa-a-bu	...	...		𒀀𒋾𒁍 a-si-bu	...	...

PARADIGM OF THE OTHER CONJUGATIONS.

	PERMANSIVE.				PRESENT.		
Iphteal ...	𒀸 𒌁 𒉌		te-sub	𒌍 𒌅 𒋛			i-ta-sab
Niphal ...	,,	,,	[nā-sub]	,,	,,		i-na-sab
Ittaphal ...	,,	,,	—	,,	,,		it-te-sab
Pael ...	,,	,,	[assab]	,,	,,		yu-as-ab, yus-sab
Iphtaal ...	,,	,,	—	,,	,,		yu-tas-sab
Shaphel ...	,,	,,	[sāsab]	,,	,,		yu-sa-sab, yu-se-sab
Istaphal ...	,,	,,	[satesab]	,,	,,		yus-te-sab, yul-te-sab
Itaphal ...	,,	,,	—	,,	,,		yu-te-sab
Pael Pass. ...	,,	,,	us-sub	,	,,		yu-us-sab
Istaphal Pass.	,,	,,	su-te-sub	,,	,,		[yus-tu-sab]

	AORIST.			IMPERATIVE.		PARTICIPLE.		
Iphteal ...	𒌍 𒌅 𒁁		i-ta-sib	[it-sib]		𒀸 𒌅 𒌋 𒁀		mu-ta-sa-bu
Niphal ...	,,	,,	i-na-sib	na-sib		,,	,,	mu-na-si-bu
Ittaphal ...	,,	,,	it-te-sib	—		,,	,,	mut-te-si-bu
Pael ...	,,	,,	yu-as-sib, yus-sib	[us-sib]		,,	,,	mus-si-bu
Iphtaal ...	,,	,,	yu-tas-sib	[i-ta-sab]		,,	,,	mut-tas-sa-bu
Shaphel ...	,,	,,	yu-sa-sib, yu-se-sib	su-sib		,,	,,	mu-se-si-bu
Istaphal ...	,,	,,	yus-te-sib, yul-te-sib	su-te-sib		,,	,,	mus-te-si-bu
Itaphal ...	,,	,.	yu-te-sib	[u-te-sib]		,,	,,	mu-te-si-bu
Pael Pass.	,,	,,	yu-us-sub	—		—		—
Istaphal Pass.	,,	,,	[yus-tu-sub]	—		—		—

Verbs פ״ה

KAL.

	PERMANSIVE. *Singular.*	PRESENT. *Singular.*	AORIST. *Singular.*
		al-lac ...	a-lic
1.	[ha-la-ca-cu]	a-lac *"I go"*	al-lic
		a-ha-bid *"I destroy"*	„ ah-bid
2. *Masc.*	[ha-la--ca-at]	„ „ tal-lac, &c. ...	„ tal-lic, &c.
2. *Fem.*	... ...	„ „ tal-la-ci ...	„ tal-li-ci
3. *Masc.*	ha-lac ...	il-lac	il-lic
3. *Fem.*	... ...	„ „ tal-lac	tal-lic
	Plural.	*Plural.*	*Plural.*
1.	... ...	„ „ na-al-lac ...	„ na-al-lic
2. *Masc.*	... ...	„ „ tal-la-cu ...	„ tal-li-cu
2. *Fem.*	... ...	„ „ tal-la-ca ...	„ tal-li-ca
3. *Masc.*	ha-la-cu	„ „ il-la-cu ...	„ il-li-cu
3. *Fem.*	[ha-la-ca] ...	„ „ il-la-ca	„ il-li-ca
	Dual.	*Dual.*	*Dual.*
3.	ha-la-ca-a ...	„ „ [illacā] ...	„ [illicā]

IMPERATIVE AND PRECATIVE.

	Singular.			*Plural.*
1.	{ lil-lic { li-lic		2. *Masc.* ...	(h)al-cu
2. *Masc.*	... ha-lic		2. *Fem.* ...	(h)al-ca
2. *Fem.*	... „ (h)al-ci		3. *Masc.* ... „ „	lil-li-cu li-li-cu
3. *Masc.*	... „ lil-lic li-lic		3. *Fem.* ... „ „	lil-li-cu, li-li-ca

INFINITIVE.	PARTICIPLE.
la-cu	(h) al - li - cu (h)a-li-cu

PARADIGM OF THE OTHER CONJUGATIONS.

PERMANSIVE.		PRESENT.			AORIST.		
Iphteal	...	𒀸 𒀹𒌋 𒐊		i-tal-lac	𒀸 𒀹𒌋 𒌋𒌋		i-tal-lic
„	...	𒁹𒁹 𒐊𒐊 𒐊		it-ta-lac	„	„	it-ta-lic
Niphal	...	[nal-luc]	„	„	i-na-al-laç	„	„	i-na-al-lic
Ittaphal	...		„	„	it-tal-lac	„	„	it-tal-lic
Pael	...	al-lac	„	„	yu-'al-lac	„	„	yu-'al-lic
„	...	„	„	„	yul-lac	„	„	yul-lic
Iphtaal	...		„	„	yu-tal-lac	„	„	yu-tal-lic
Shaphel	...	[sal-lac]	„	„	yu-sal-lac	„	„	yu-sal-lic
Istaphel	...		„	„	yus-tal-lac	„	„	yus-tal-lic

IMPERATIVE.			PARTICIPLE.		
Iphteal	...	[it-lic]	𒀸 𒀹𒌋 𒐊𒐊 𒐊		mu-tal-la-cu
Niphal	...	na-al-lic	„	,	mu-na-al-li-cu
Ittaphal	...		„	„	mut-tal-li-cu
Pael	...	(h)ul-lic	„	„	mu-'al-li-cu
Iphtaal	...	[i-tal-lic]	„	„	mu-tal-li-cu
Shaphal	...	sul-lic	„	„	mu-sal-li-cu
Istaphal	...	[su-tal-lic]	„	„	mus-tal-li-cu

Verbs פ״י.

KAL.

PERMANSIVE.	PRESENT.	AORIST.	IMPERATIVE AND PRECATIVE.
Singular.	*Singular.*	*Singular.*	*Singular.*
I.　[u-la-da-cu]	𒁹𒁹 u-lad	𒁹𒁹 u-lid, "*I begat*"	𒁹𒁹 lu-lid
2. *Masc.*　…　…	„　„　tu-lad	„　„　tu-lid	„　„　lid
2. *Fem.*　…　…	„　„　tu-la-di	„　„　tu-li-di	„　„　li-di
3. *Masc.*　[u-lid]　…	𒁹𒁹 yu-lad	𒁹𒁹 yu-lid	„　„　lu-lid
3. *Fem.*　…　…	„　„　tu-lad	„　„　tu-lid	
Plural.	*Plural.*	*Plural.*	*Plural.*
I.　…　…	„　„　nu-lad	„　„　nu-lid	
2. *Masc.*　…　…	„　„　tu-la-du	„　„　tu-li-du	„　„　li-du
2. *Fem.*　…　…	„　„　tu-la-da	„　„　tu-li-da	„　„　li-da
3. *Masc.*　…　…	„　„　yu-la-du	„　„　yu-li-du	„　„　lu-li-du
3. *Fem.*　…　…	„　„　yu-la-da	„　„　yu-li-da	„　„　lu-li-da
Dual	*Dual.*	*Dual.*	
3.　…　…	„　„　[yu-la-da-a]	„　„　[yulidā]	

INFINITIVE.	PARTICIPLE.
𒁹 a-la-du	𒁹 u-li-du
𒁹 lā-du	𒁹 a-li-du.

PARADIGM OF THE OTHER CONJUGATIONS.

	PERMANSIVE.	PRESENT.		AORIST.	
Iphteal …	[telud]	𒁹 i-tu-lad		𒁹 i-tu-lid	
Niphal …	[nulud]	„　„　[i-ne-lad]		„　„　[i-ne-lid]	
Ittaphal …		„　„　i-tu-lad		„　„　it-tu-lid	
Pael …	[ullad]	„　„ { yu-'ul-lad / yul-lad }		„　„ { yu-'ul-lid / yul-lid }	
Iphtaal …		„　„　yu-tul-lad		„　„　yu-tul-lid	
Shaphel …	[sulad]	„　„　yu-se-lad		„　„　yu-se-lid	
Istaphal …	[sutelad]	„　„　yus-te-lad		„　„　yus-te lid	

IMPERATIVE.		PARTICIPLE.	
Iphteal	...	𒀸 𒂍𒐊 𒂍𒅗 𒁁	mu-ta-li-du
Niphal	... nu-lid	,, ,,	mu-ne-li-du
Ittaphal	...	,, ,,	mut-te-li-du
Pael	... ul-lid	,, ,,	mul-li-du, mu-li-du
Iphtaal	...	𒌋𒀀 𒀹 𒄿𒐊 𒂍 𒁁	mut-te-el-la-du
Shaphel	... su-lid	,, ,,	mu-sa-li-du, mus-te-li-du
Istaphal	... [su-te-lid]	𒂍𒐊 𒀹 𒂍𒅗 𒁁	mus-te-li-du

Verbs פ״י.

KAL.

PERMANSIVE.	PRESENT.	AORIST.	IMPERATIVE AND PRECATIVE.
Singular.	*Singular.*	*Singular.*	*Singular.*
1. [inikacu]	𒀀𒈾𒀝 i-na-ak	𒀀𒉌𒅅 i-ni-ik "*I suckled*"	𒇷𒉌𒅅 li-nik
2. *Masc.* ...	„ „ ti-na-ak	„ „ ti-ni-ik	„ „ nik
2. *Fem.* ...	„ „ ti-na-ki	„ „ ti-ni-ki	„ „ ni-ki
3. *Masc.* ...	„ „ i-nak	„ „ i-nik	„ „ li-nik
3. *Fem.* ...	„ „ ti-nak	„ „ ti-nik	...
Plural.	*Plural.*	*Plural.*	*Plural.*
1.	„ „ ni-nak	„ „ ni-nik	...
2. *Masc.* ...	„ „ ti-na-ku	„ „ ti-ni-ku	„ „ ni-ku
2. *Fem.* ...	„ „ ti-na-ka	„ „ ti-ni-ka	„ „ ni-ka
3. *Masc.* [inikú]	„ „ i-na-ku	„ „ i-ni-ku	„ „ li-ni-ku
3. *Fem.* ...	„ „ i-na-ka	„ „ i-ni-ka	„ „ li-ni-ka

PARTICIPLE.

𒀀𒉌𒆪 i-ni-ku

PARADIGM OF THE OTHER CONJUGATIONS.

PERMANSIVE.	PRESENT.	AORIST.
Iphteal ... [tenuk]	𒀀𒋾𒈾𒀝 i-ti-na-ak	𒀀𒋾𒅅 i-ti-nik
Niphal ... [nenuk]	„ „ i-ni-na-ak	„ „ i-ni-nik
Ittaphal ...	„ „ it-ti-nak	„ „ it-ti-nik
Pael ... [ennak]	„ „ i-en-nak	„ „ i-en-nik
	„ „ in-nak	„ „ in-nik
Iphtaal ...	„ „ yut-te-en-nak	„ „ yut-te-en-nik
Shaphel ... [senak]	„ „ yu-se-nak	„ „ yu-se-nik
Istaphal ... [satenak]	„ „ yus-te-nak	„ „ yus-te-nik
Istataphal... [satetinak]	𒁹𒀀𒀀𒀀 yus-te-te-nak	„ „ yus-te-te-nik

IMPERATIVE.				PARTICIPLE.	
Iphteal	...	[it-nik]	...		mu-ti-ni-ku
Niphal	...	ni-nik	...	,, ,,	mu-ni-ni-ku
Ittaphal	...	[ni-ti-nik]	...	,, ,,	mu-te-ni-ku
Pael	...	un-nik	...	,, ,,	mu-en-ni-ku
Iphtaal	...	it-tin-nik	...	,, ,,	mut-te-en-ni-ku
Shaphel	...	su-nik	...	,, ,,	mu-se-ni-ku
Istaphal	...	su-te-nik	...	,, ,,	mus-te-ni-ku
Istataphal	...	[su-te-te-nik]		,, ,,	[mus-te-te-ni-ku]

N.B.—All these verbs are greatly confounded with one another, and had also a tendency to adopt forms borrowed from verbs ע״פ, consequently the same verb (e.g. *asabu*) might have some forms which presupposed a verb פ׳א, others which presupposed a verb פ״ו (*usabu*), others which presupposed a verb פ״ן (*nasabu*), &c. Thus the precative *lusib*, *lusibu* given above comes not from *asabu* (verb פ״א), but from *usabu* (verb פ״ו).

Verbs ע״פ:—

KAL.

	PERMANSIVE.		PRESENT.	
	Singular.		*Singular.*	
1.	...	[epsacu]	e-pa-as, ep-pas	"*I make*"
2. *Masc.*	...	[epsat]	te-pa-as, &c.	
2. *Fem.*	...	—	te-pa-si	
3. *Masc.*	...	e-pis	e-pa-as	
3. *Fem.*	...	—	te-pa-as	
	Plural.		*Plural.*	
1.	...	—	ne-pa-as	
2. *Masc.*	...	—	te-pa-su	
2. *Fem.*	...	—	te-pa-sa	
3. *Masc.*	...	[e-pi-su]	e-pa-su	
3. *Fem.*	...	e-pi-sa	e-pa-sa	
	Dual.		*Dual.*	
3.		[episā]	[epasā]	

	AORIST.			IMPERATIVE AND PRECATIVE.
	Singular.			*Singular.*
1.	...	e-pus	e-mid "*I stood*"	li-pus
2. *Masc.*	...	te-pus	te-mid	e-pus
2. *Fem.*	...	te-pu-si	te-mi-di	e-pu-si
3. *Masc.*	...	e-pus	e-mid	li-pus
3. *Fem.*	...	te-pus	te-mid	—
	Plural.			*Plural.*
1.	...	ne-pus	ne-mid	—
2. *Masc.*	...	te-pu-su	te-mi-du	e-pu-su
2. *Fem.*	...	te-pu-sa	te-mi-da	e-pu-sa
3. *Masc.*	...	e-pu-su	e-mi-du	li-pu-su
3. *Fem.*	...	e-pu-sa	e-mi-da	li-pu-sa
	Dual.			
3.	...	[epusā	emidā]	

INFINITIVE.		PARTICIPLE.
e-pi-su a-pū-su "*to make*"		e-pi-su

PARADIGM OF THE OTHER CONJUGATIONS.

	PERMANSIVE.			PRESENT.		AORIST.	
Iphteal ...	𒅗𒁹	et-pus	𒂊𒁹	e-tap-pas	𒂊𒁹	e-te-pus
Niphal ...	,,	,,	[nebus]		ip-pas, i-pas	,,	,,	ip-pis, i-pis
Ittaphal...	,,	,,	[netepus]		it-te-pas	,,	,,	it-te-pis
Pael ...	,,	,,	[eppas]		yup-pas	,,	,,	yup-pis
Iphtaal ...	,,	,,	—		yu-te-ip-pas	,,	,,	yu-te-ip-pis
Shaphel ...	,,	,,	[sepas]		yu-se-pas	,,	,,	yu-se-pis
Istaphal...	,,	,,	[satepas]		yus-te-pas	,,	,,	yus-te-pis

	IMPERATIVE.			PARTICIPLE.	
Iphteal ...		et-pis		mu-te-pi-su
Niphal ...	,,	,,	ni-ip-pis		mu-ne-pi-su
Ittaphal ...	,,	,,	ni-te-pis		mu-te-pa-su
Pael ...		up-pis		mup-pi-su
Iphtaal ...	,,	,,	—		mut-te-ip-pi-su
Shaphel ...	,,	,,	su-pis		mu-si-pi-su
Istaphal ...	,,	,,	su-ut-te-pis		mus-te-pi-su

The Babylonian dialect had 𒂊𒁹 *i-bus* or 𒂊𒁹 *e-i-bus*, *i-bas* or *e-i-bas*, *i-bu-su* or *e-i-bu-su*, and *i-ba-su* or *e-i-ba-su*, instead of the 3rd pers. sing. and pl. forms given above. [A Babylonian *b* often represented an Assyrian *p*.] The Babylonian dialect also said 𒂊𒁹 *yu-'ub-bas*, &c., instead of the contracted *yubbas*, &c.

CONCAVE VERBS.

KAL.

	PERMANSIVE. Singular.			PRESENT. Singular.	
1.	𒀀𒈠𒋢	ca-ma-cu *"I rise"*		a-tar	
	𒀀𒀀𒈾𒋢	ca'-a-na-cu, *"I establish"*		at-tar *"I bring back"*	
2. *Masc.*	„	„	[camat, ca'anat]	„ „	ta-tar, &c.
2. *Fem.*	—	—		„ „	ta-ta-ri
3. *Masc.*	𒅗𒄠	ca-am		„ „	i-tar
„	𒅗𒅔	ca-in		„ „	„
3. *Fem.*	„ „	[camat] [ca-i-nat]		„ „	ta-tar

	Plural.			Plural.	
1.	—	—		„ „	na-tar
2. *Masc.*	—	—		„ „	ta-ta-ru
2. *Fem.*	—	—		„ „	ta-ta-ra
3. *Masc.*	𒅗𒈬	ca-mu, ca-i-nu		„ „	i-ta-ru
3. *Fem.*	„ „	ca-ma, ca-i-na		„ „	i-ta-ra

	Dual.			Dual.	
3.	𒅗𒈠	camā		„ „	i-ta-ra-a

AORIST.

	Singular.				Plural.			
1.	a-tur, at-tur		a-ciś *"I cut off"*		na-tur		na-ciś	
2. *Masc.*	„	ta-tur, &c.	„	ta-ciś	„	ta-tu-ru	„	ta-ci-śu
2. *Fem.*	„	ta-tu-ri	„	ta-ci-śi	„	ta-tu-ra	„	ta-ci-śa
3. *Masc.*	„	i-tur	„	i-ciś	„	i-tu-ru	„	i-ci-śu
3. *Fem.*	„	ta-tur	„	ta-ciś	„	i-ta-ra	„	i-ci-śa

			Dual.			
3.	„	i-tu-ra-a	„	i-ci-śa-a		

KAL.—*continued*.

IMPERATIVE AND PRECATIVE.

Singular.			Plural.	
1.	𒀭 𒀭 𒀭 lu-ut-tur, lu-tur-ru			
2. *Masc.*	𒀭 tir, tir-ra ⟶ tar		𒀭 du-ku "*smite ye;*" cinu "*establish ye*"	
	𒀭 cin 𒀭 duk			
2. *Fem.*	„ ti-ri, ta-ri, ci-ni, du-ci		„ du-cā, ci-nā	
3. *M. and F.*	„ lit-tur, li-tur		„ lit-tu-ru, li-tu-ru	
			Dual.	
			„ lit-tu-ra, li-tu-ra	

INFINITIVE.

𒀭 𒀭 𒀭 ta'-a-ru *to turn*

PARTICIPLE ACT.

𒀭 𒀭 𒀭 ta'-i-ru   𒀭 𒀭 𒀭 ca'-i-nu

PARTICIPLE PASS.

𒀭 𒀭 ti-ru   𒀭 𒀭 di-ku   𒀭 𒀭 ci-nu

PARADIGM OF THE OTHER CONJUGATIONS.

	PERMANSIVE.			PRESENT.	
Iphteal.	𒀭 𒀭 𒀭	{ te-bā-cu "*I come*" / [te-cin]	𒀭 𒀭 𒀭	ic-ta-an	
			𒀭 𒀭 𒀭	it-ba-a	
Niphalel ...	„ „	[na-ac-nu-un]	„ „	ic-ca-na-an	
Ittaphalel ...	„ „	[na-ac-te-nun]	„ „	it-tac-na-an	
Pael ...	𒀭 𒀭 𒀭	ci-i-in	„ „	{ yu-uc-ca-an / yuc-ca-an	
Iphtael ...	„ „	—	„ „	yuc-ta-an	
Palel ...	𒀭 𒀭 𒀭	cu-un-nu, *3rd pl.*	„ „	yuc-na-an	
Iphtalel ...	„ „	—	„ „	ic-te-na-an	
Shaphel ...	„ „	[sa-ca-in]	„ „	yu-sa-ca-an	
Istaphal ...	„ „	[sa-te-ca-an]	„ „	yus-ta-ca-an	
Aphel ...	„ „	—	„ „	yu-ca-(y)an	
Itaphal ...	„ „	—	„ „	yuc-ca-an	
Shaphael ...	„ „	[saccen]	„ „	yu-sac-ca-an	
Istaphael ...	„ „	—	„ „	yus-tac-ca-an	
Shaphel Pass.	„ „	[su-cu-un]	𒀭 𒀭 𒀭 𒀭	yu-su-ca-an	

PARADIGM OF THE OTHER CONJUGATIONS.

	AORIST.		IMPERATIVE.	PARTICIPLE.	
Iphteal	... 〔cuneiform〕 ic-ti-in, 〔cuneiform〕 it-bu'		[ci-tu-un], [te-bu]	〔cuneiform〕	mu-uc-ti-nu
Niphalel	... ,, ,,	ic-ca-nin / iz-za-nun	na-ac-nin	,, ,,	mu-uc-ca-ni-nu
Ittaphalel	... ,, ,,	it-tac-nin	ni-tac-nin	,, ,,	mut-tac-na-nu
Pael	... ,, ,,	yu-uc-cin / yuc-cin	[uc-cin]	,, ,,	mu-uc-ci-nu
Iphteal	... ,, ,,	yuc-ti-in	—	,, ,,	mu-tac-ci-nu
Palel	... ,, ,,	yuc-ni-in	uc-ni-in	,, ,,	mu-uc-ti-nu
Iphtalel	... ,, ,,	ic-te-nin	—	,, ,,	—
Shaphel	... ,, ,,	yu-sa-cin	su-cu-un	,, ,,	mu-sa-ci-nu
Istaphel	... ,, ,,	yus-ta-cin	su-ut-cu-un	,, ,,	mu-sac-ci-nu
Aphel	... ,, ,,	yu-cin	cin, cu-un	,, ,,	mu-ci-nu
Itaphal	... ,, ,,	yuc-cin	—	,, ,,	mu-uc-ci-nu
Shaphael	... ,, ,,	yu-sac-cin	su-uc-cu-un	,, ,,	mu-sac-ci-nu
Istaphael	... ,, ,,	[yus-tac-cin]	—	,, ,,	mus-tac-ci-nu
Shaphel Pass.	〔cuneiform〕	yu-su-cin	—	,, ,,	—

It will be noticed that Palel and Iphtalel regularly appear in these Concave Verbs, and that Niphalel and Ittaphalel take the place of Niphal and Ittaphal.

The permansive of Pael changes *ayya* into *i*, and has a passive or neuter signification.

Verbs ל"א, ל"ה, ל"ו, ל"י, ל"ע.

KAL.

	PERMANSIVE (or Perfect).	PRESENT.	AORIST.
	Singular.	*Singular.*	*Singular.*
1.	𒈾𒊓𒆪 na-sa-cu "I lift up"	𒀀𒃮𒁉 a-gab-bi' "I speak"	𒀝𒁉 ag-bi' — 𒀊𒉡 ab-nu' "I built"
2. *Masc.*	𒈾𒊓𒀜 na-sa-at …	,, ,, ta-gab-bi'…	,, tag-bi' ,, tab-nu
2. *Fem.*	— — …	,, ,, ta-gab-bi'	,, tag-bi' ,, tab-nu
3. *Masc.*	𒈾𒋢 na-su …	,, ,, i-gab-bi' …	,, ig-bi' ,, ib-nu'
3. *Fem.*	𒈾𒊍 na-sat …	,, ,, ta-gab-bi'	,, tag-bi' ,, tab-nu'
	Plural.	*Plural.*	*Plural.*
1.	— — …	,, ,, na-gab-bi'	,, nag-bi' ,, nab-nu
2. *Masc.*	— — …	,, ,, ta-gab-bu	,, tag-bu ,, tab-nu
2. *Fem.*	— — …	,, ,, ta-gab-ba	,, tag-ba ,, tab-na
3. *Masc.*	𒈾𒋢𒌋 na-su-u …	,, , i-gab-bu …	,, ig-bu ,. ib-nu
3. *Fem.*	𒈾𒊓𒀀 na-sa-a …	,, ,, i-gab-ba …	,. ig-ba ,, ib-na
	Dual.	*Dual.*	*Dual.*
3.	𒈾𒊓𒀀 na-sa-a …	,, ,, i-gab-ba-a	,, ig-ba-a ,, ib-na-a

IMPERATIVE AND PRECATIVE.			INFINITIVE.
	Singular.		𒁀𒉡 ba-nu " to build"
1.	𒇻�-bi' lu-ug-bi' 𒇻𒀊𒉡 lu-ub-nu'		𒂵𒀀𒁍 ga-a-bu " to speak"
2. *Masc.*	,, ,, ba-ni, ba-an ,, ,, khi-dhi'		𒈾𒀀𒋢 na-a-su " to lift"
2. *Fem.*	,, ,, ba-ni-i ,, ,, khi-dhi-i		
3. *Masc.*	,, ,, li-ig-bi' ,, , li-ib-nu'		PARTICIPLE.
	Plural.		𒁀𒉡 ba-nu
2. *Masc.*	,, ,, ba-nu-u		𒂵𒁍 ga-bu
2. *Fem.*	,. ,, ba-na-a		
3. *Masc.*	,, ,, li-ib-nu-u		
3. *Fem.*	,, ,, lib-na-a		

Verbs ל״ע properly have *e* in the last syllable, as *is-me-e* "he heard," but *i* frequently takes its place. In the plural we may have *is-me-u* as well as *is-mu.*

PARADIGM OF THE OTHER CONJUGATIONS.

PERMANSIVE.				PRESENT.		
Iphteal ...			[kitbu']			ik-te-ba'
Pael			[kabba']	„	„	yu-kab-ba'
Iphtaal ...			—	„	„	yuk-tăb-ba'
Niphal ...			nak-bu'	„	„	ik-ka-ba'
Ittaphal ...	„	„	[nak-te-bu']	„	„	it-tak-ba'
Niphael ...	„	„	[nakabbu']	„	„	it-kab-ba'
Shaphel ...	„	„	[sakba']	„	„	yu-sak-ba'
Istaphal ...	„	„	[satkeba']	„	„	yus-te-ik-ba'
Shaphael ...	„	„	[sakabba']	„	„	yus-kab-ba'
Istaphael ...	„	„	[satkabba']	„	„	yus-kab-ba'
Shaphel Pass...			ku-ub-bu'	„	„	yu-ku-ub-ba'

AORIST.				IMPERATIVE.		
Iphteal ...			ik-te-bi'			kit-bi'
Pael	„	„	yu-kab-bi'	„	„	ku-ub-bi'
Iphtaal ...	„	„	yuk-tab-bi'	„	„	ki-tib-bi'
Niphal ...	„	„	ik-ka-bi'	„	„	nak-bi'
Ittaphal ...	„	„	it-tak-bi'	„	„	ni-tak-bi'
Niphael ...	„	„	ik-kab-bi'	„	„	[na-kab-bi']
Shaphel ...	„	„	yu-sak-bi'	„	„	suk-bu'
Istaphal ...	„	„	yus-te-ik-bi'	„	„	su-te-ik-bi'
Shaphael ...	„	„	yus-kab-bi'	„	„	[su-ku-ub-bu']
Istaphael ...	„	„	yus-kab-bi'	„	„	[su-te-ku-ub-bi']
Shaphel Pass...	„	„	yu-ku-ub-bi'			—

PARTICIPLE.

Iphteal...			muk-te-bu-u	*Niphael*...			muk-kab-bu-u
Pael ...	„	„	mu-kab-bu-u	*Shaphel*...	„	„	mu-sak-bu-u
Iphtaal	„	„	muk-tab-bu-u	*Istaphal*	„	„	mus-te-ik-bu-u
Niphal...	„	„	muk-ka-bu-u	*Shaphael*	„	„	mus-kab-bu-u
Ittaphal	„	„	mut-tak-bu-u	*Istaphael*	„	„	mus-te-kab-bu-u

By combining the forms given in these Paradigms the student will be able to obtain the forms of *doubly defective Verbs* like 𒀀𒁍𒂊 *atsu* "to go forth," 𒆠𒌋 *lavu* "to cling to," 𒂊𒌋 *bavu* "to come."

PARADIGM OF QUADRILITERAL VERBS.

The Characters to be added by the Student.

	PERMANSIVE.				PRESENT.	
Kal (=*Palel*) ...	𒁹𒋫𒀭		pal-cit		{ i-pal-cat	" *he crosses* " }
					{ iś-khu-par	" *he overthrows* " }
Iphtalel	,,	,,	[pitlucut]	𒁹𒐏 𒀭	yup-tal-cat	
Saphalel	,,	,,	[saplacat]	,,	,,	yus-pal-cat
Istaphalel	,,	,,	[saptelcat]	,,	,,	yus-ta-pal-cat
Niphalel	,,	,,	[naplacut]	,,	,,	ip-pal-cat
Ittaphalel	,,	,,	[naptelcut]	,,	,,	it-ta-pal-cat
Niphalla	,,	,,	—	,,	,,	ip-pal-ca-ta-at

	AORIST.	IMPERATIVE.	PARTICIPLE.
Kal (=*Palel*)	{ i-pal-cit, i-pa-la-cit } { ip-la-cit, iś-khu-pir }	pal-cit	mu-pal-ci-tu
Iphtalel ...	yup-tal-cit	pi-tal-cat	mu-up-tal-ci-tu
Saphalel ...	yus-pal-cit	su-pal-cut	mu-pal-ci-tu
Istaphalel ...	yus-ta-pal-cit	sit-pal-cut	mus-ta-pal-ci-tu
Niphalel ...	{ ip-pal-cit } { ip-par-sud " *he pur-sued* " }	ni-pal-cat	mu-up-pal-ci-tu
Ittaphalel ...	it-ta-pal-cit	[na-te-pal-cat]	mut-ta-pal-ci-tu
Niphalla ...	𒁹𒋫𒀭𒂊 ip-pal-cit-it	... ...	mu-up-pal-cit-tu

VERBS TO BE CONJUGATED BY THE STUDENT.

1.	𒈪𒌋𒌋	ca-sa-du	*to obtain*	21.	𒈪𒌋𒌋	*to extend*
2.	𒈪𒌋𒌋	na-ba-lu	*to fall, destroy*	22.	𒈪𒌋𒌋	*to proclaim*
3.	𒈪𒌋𒌋	pa-ra-tsu	*to speak falsely*	23.	𒈪𒌋𒌋	*to cut off*
4.	𒈪𒌋𒌋	tsa-ba-tu	*to take*	24.	𒈪𒌋𒌋	*to slay*
5.	𒈪𒌋𒌋	sa-dha-ru	*to write*	25.	𒈪𒌋𒌋	*to oversee*
6.	𒈪𒌋𒌋	sa-pa-ru	*to send*	26.	𒈪𒌋𒌋	*to make bricks.*
7.	𒈪𒌋𒌋	ma'-a-tu	*to die*	27.	𒈪𒌋𒌋	*to thresh*
8.	𒈪𒌋𒌋	sa-la-dhu	*to rule*	28.	𒈪𒌋𒌋	*to measure*
9.	𒈪𒌋𒌋	ba-kha-ru	*to choose*	29.	𒈪𒌋𒌋	*to pour*
10.	𒈪𒌋𒌋	na-ca-ru	*to be strange*			

Verbs to be transliterated and conjugated by the Student.

Verbs to be conjugated and the Characters added by the Student.

11.	𒈪𒌋𒌋		*to protect*	30.	ca-ra-bu	*to be near*
12.	𒈪𒌋𒌋		*to complete*	31.	ka-a-su	*to snare*
13.	𒈪𒌋𒌋		*to collect*	32.	e-bi-lu	*to be lord*
14.	𒈪𒌋𒌋		*to finish*	33.	ha-pa-cu	*to smite*
15.	𒈪𒌋𒌋		*to hear*	34.	ma-la-cu	*to rule*
16.	𒈪𒌋𒌋		*to trust*	35.	ca-na-su	*to submit*
17.	𒈪𒌋𒌋		*to destroy*	36.	ma-kha-ru	*to be present, to receive*
18.	𒈪𒌋𒌋		*to cross over*	37.	sa-ra-cu	*to deliver*
19.	𒈪𒌋𒌋		*to curse*	38.	na-du-u	*to place*
20.	𒈪𒌋𒌋		*to ask*	39.	za-ca-ru	*to remember*
				40.	a-ba-lu	*to bring*

VERBS *to be conjugated and the Characters added by the Student.*

1.	e-ri-bu ...	*to descend*	59.		e-zi-bu ...	*to forsake*
2.	e-lu-u ...	*to ascend*	60.		pa-ta-khu	*to cut open*
3.	e-ci-mu ...	*to strip, to take*	61.		ga-ru-u ...	*to war*
4.	sa-la-lu ...	*to spoil*	62.		sa-ca-ru...	*to drink*
5.	khar-pa-su	*to be violent*	63.		ra-tsa-pu	*to build*
6.	ca-vu-u ...	*to burn*	64.			*to build*
7.	sa-tu-u ...	*to drink*	65.			*to go*
8.	sa-la-pu...	*to pull out*	66.			*to hate*
9.	ka-lu-u ...	*to burn*	67.			*to see*
10.	na-ca-ru	*to dig*	68.			*to fill*
11.	ma-lu-u ...	*to fill*	69.			*to die*
12.	śa-kha-ru	*to go round*	70.			*to assemble*
13.	e-ni-khu	*to decay*	71.			*to burn*
14.	pa-ra-ru	*to crush*	72.			*to learn*
15.	kha-ba-tu	*to devastate*	73.			*to make*
16.	par-sa-du	*to fly*	74.			*to conquer*
.	ta-ra-tsu	*to arrange*	75.			*to be good*
.	na-pa-ra-cu	*to break*				

LIST OF ASSYRIAN PREPOSITIONS.

1. 𒌋𒌋 𒀭𒌋, 𒄿𒐀	a-di ...	*up to*	18. 𒀭𒌅	im ...	*from, with*
2. 𒌋𒌋 𒀭	a-khi, a-kha-at	*at the side of*	19. 𒂊𒀀𒀀; 𒀀	ina, in ...	*in, by, with*
3. 𒌋𒌋 𒀭𒂷	a-khar ...	*behind*	20. 𒃲𒅆 𒀀𒀀	in-na, in-nannu	*in, from*
4. 𒌋𒌋 𒀀𒀀, 𒀀	a-na, an	*to, for*	21. 𒀁𒀀 𒆠	it-ti, it ...	*with, during*
5. 𒐕𒀀𒌋𒐕 𒁺	ar-cu, ar-ci	*after*	22. 𒁹	ci ...	*according to, as*
6. 𒀸 𒂊𒀀	as-su, as-sum	*in, by, in regard to*	23. 𒁹 𒂊𒀀	ci-ma, cim	*like*
7. 𒄭𒀀 𒁁	ba-lu, baliv	*without*	24. 𒁹 𒌋𒌋𒌋𒌋	ci-bit ...	*by command of*
8. 𒐕 𒂅	bi-rid ...	*within, near*	25. 𒁹 𒌋𒌋𒌋	ci-rib ...	*in the midst of*
9. 𒀭𒌋 𒀭	di-khi ...	*opposite*	26. 𒁁 𒂊𒌋𒌋𒌋	cu-um ...	*instead of*
10. 𒀭𒌋𒌋 𒃲𒂊𒀀	ul-li ...	*among*	27. 𒂊𒀀 𒋼 𒅗	la-pa-ni...	*before*
11. 𒀭𒌋𒌋 𒂊𒀀 𒌋𒌋 𒊹	ul-lā-nu	*before*	28. 𒃲𒂊𒀀 𒀀 𒆠	li-me-ti, li	*near*
12. 𒀭𒌋𒌋𒂊𒀭𒐕𒂊	ul-la-num-ma	*upon*	29. 𒀾𒌋𒌋 𒐕	lib-bi, libba	*in the midst of*
13. 𒀭𒌋𒌋 𒃲𒂊𒀀	ul-tu ...	*from, out of*	30. 𒂊𒌋𒌋 𒄿𒀀𒐕	makh-ri	*before*
14. 𒂊𒌋𒌋 𒃲𒂊𒀀	is-tu ...	*from, out of*	31. 𒀭𒆳 𒀭𒂊𒐖𒌋𒌋𒌋	mi-ikh-rit	*among*
15. 𒅋𒌋𒌋𒌋 𒂊𒀀 𒈦	il-la-mu...	*before*	32. 𒀭𒆳	nir ...	*below, near, against*
16. 𒅋𒌋𒌋𒌋 𒂊𒀀 𒄿𒀀	il-la-an [*or* elan]	*beyond*	33. 𒋾 𒀭𒆳 𒂊𒀀	ne-mi-du	*towards*
17. 𒅋𒌋𒌋𒌋 𒁁	il-lu ...	*upon*	34. 𒂊𒌋 𒀭𒂷 𒆠	śi-khar-ti	*throughout*
			35. 𒂅𒌋 𒂊𒀀	e-la ...	*over*

ASSYRIAN PREPOSITIONS—*continued.*

36.	e-la-at ...	*except*	41.	pa-ni, pan	*before*
37.	e-li, el ...	*over, upon, above, beside*	42.	tsir ...	*against, upon*
			43.	sa ...	*of, in regard to*
38.	e-la-an ...	*beyond*	44.	sap-tu ...	*by the help of*
39	e-ma ...	*around*	45.	se-pu ...	*under*
40.	er-ti ...	*against*	46.	tic ...	*behind*

THE COMPOUND PREPOSITIONS.

1.		a-na it-ti	*to be with*
2.		a-na la	*not to be*
3.		a-na im	*to*
4.		a-na e-li	*over*
5.		a-na er-ti	*to the presence of*
6.		ul-tu ci-rib	*from the midst of*
7.		ul-tu lib-bi	*from the midst of*
8.		ul-tu pa-ni	*from before*
9.		i-na bi-bil, i-na bi-ib-lat	*in the midst of*
10.		i-na a-di dhe-mi	*by command of*
11.		i-na ci-rib	*in the midst of*
12.		i-na lib-bi	*in the midst of*
13.		i-na śu-ki	*in front of*
14.		i-na ni-rib	*near to*
15.		i-na la	*for want of*
16.		i-na pan	*from before*
17.		i-na e-li	*above*
18.		i-na er-ti	*after*
19.		i-na tir-tsi, i-na tar-tsi	*in the {presence/time} of*
20.		i-na an-ni	*at this time*
21.		ci la	*without*
		&c., &c.	

THE CONJUNCTIONS.

1. 𒀸 or 𒀸𒁲	u or vā	and (between nouns and clauses)	12. 𒂍𒅀	ma-a ...	that, for umma (see Adverbs)
𒂍	vă ...	and (after verbs)	13. 𒅆	sa ...	when, because, where, that
2. 𒀸, 𒂍	û ...	or	14. 𒐊𒂍	sum-ma	if, thus, when
3. 𒅀 𒅀	ai ...	not (with the Imperat. or Precat.)	15. 𒀠𒆷 𒂍 𒅆	al-la sa	after that
4. 𒀠𒁲 𒌋	ac-ca	how?	16. 𒅀 𒀀𒁲 𒅆	a-di-sa, a-di e-li sa	in so far as, while
5. 𒌋𒈬	im ...	if			
6. 𒀸𒋢	as-su	when, meanwhile, now	17. 𒅈𒋛 𒅆	ar-ci sa	after that
7. 𒄿𒉡	i-nu...	behold, now	18. 𒌋𒈬 𒂍 𒈠 𒂍	im ma-ti-ma	if at all
8. 𒆠	cī ...	when, thus, as, while	19. 𒄿𒈾 𒈠 𒂍	i-na ma-ti-ma	in any case
9. 𒆠𒈠	ci-ma	as, thus			
10. 𒆷	lā ...	not	20. 𒆠 𒅆	ci-sa ...	whenever
𒌌	ul ...	not (with verbs)	21. 𒇷𒁍 𒅆	lib-bu sa	just as
11. 𒈝	lū ...	whether, or, truly (verbal prefix of past time)	22. 𒅆 𒂍 𒈠𒋛𒈠	sa ma-ti-ma	of what place?

THE ADVERBS.

The most common mode of forming the adverb in Assyrian was by attaching the termination -*is* to the construct-state of a noun (whether sing. or pl.) ; as *rab-is* "greatly," *el-is* "above," *sallat-is* "for a spoil," *caccab-is* "like a star," *sadan-is* "like mountains." The accusative case of the noun, with or without the mimmation, might also be used adverbially, as *palcā* "amply," *rubam* "greatly."

The genitive also, with or without the mimmation, is sometimes found ; as *batstsi* "in ruin," *labirim* "of old."

The most common adverbs of place and time are the following :—

1.	𒀀𒂵𒈾	a-gan-na ...	*here*	11.	ci-ha-am ...	*thus*
2.	𒀀𒁲	a-di ...	*till*	12.	lu-ma(h)-du	*much*
3.		ai-um-ma, ya-um-ma, um-ma	*never*	13.	makh-ri ...	*formerly*
		.... la		14.	ma-te-ma...	*in times past*
4.		al-lu, al-la, al-la sa	*then, afterwards*	15.	e-nin-na ...	*again*
				16.	e-nu-va ...	*when, at that time*
5.		ar-ci ...	*afterwards*	17.	pa-na-ma...	*formerly*
6.		u-di-na ...	*at the same [time]*	18.	tsa-tis ...	*in future*
				19.	sa... ...	*when*
7.		um-ma ...	*thus, that*	20.	sa-num-ma, sa-nam-ma	*in a foreign land, elsewhere*
8.		ul-lā-na, ultu ulla	*from that time, from of old*			
				21.	ina yumi suma	*at that time*
9.		zi-is ...	*as of old*			
10.		ca-la-ma ...	*of all kinds*	22.	um-maas-su	*because*

DERIVATION OF NOUNS.

A large proportion of Assyrian nouns are derived from different forms of the verb. Thus from Kal we have the infinitives ⟦cuneiform⟧ *ra-kha-a-tsu* "to inundate," ⟦cuneiform⟧ *ni-ci-i-śu* "to cut off," and ⟦cuneiform⟧ *u-mu-u-ru* "to keep;" the participle passive ⟦cuneiform⟧ *da-li-i-khu* "troubled," and the active participle ⟦cuneiform⟧ *ma-a-li-cu* "ruling" where he long *ā* of the first syllable serves to distinguish it from *mă-li-cu* "a king," which is derived from the Permansive.

From Pael we have nouns like ⟦cuneiform⟧ *kar-ra-du* "war-like," *im-mu-nu* "injured."

From Palel, ⟦cuneiform⟧ *nam-ri-ri* "bright."

From Iphteal and Iphtaal, ⟦cuneiform⟧ *cit-ru-bu* "a meeting," *lat-bu-su* clothed," *git-ma-lu* "a benefactor."

From Shaphel, ⟦cuneiform⟧ *sap-sa-ku* "an opening," *sum-cu-tu* "a laughter."

From Niphal, ⟦cuneiform⟧ *nab-kha-ru* "collected," *nab-ni-tu* "offspring," *um-kha-ru* "a receipt."

From the weak verbs come words like ⟦cuneiform⟧ *mi-ru* "offspring" for *na'-iru, sa-hu* "summit" from *nasu*, and from verbs י″פ, *lit-tu* (for *lid-tu*), *li-du, i-i-tu, li-da-a-tu*, and *lit-tu-tu*, all meaning "offspring." Also forms which repeat he second radical, as *li-lic-cu* "a going," *lil-li-du* "a birth," *dadmu* "man," the Heb. *adam* אדם.

When a monosyllable is repeated the last consonant of the first syllable is enerally assimilated to the first consonant of the second syllable, as ⟦cuneiform⟧ *ak-ka-du* (for *kad-kadu*) "a head," *ca-ac-ca-bu* (for *cab-cabu*) "a star."

The prefix *M* denotes the instrument, action, or place, as ⟦cuneiform⟧ *man-za-zu* "bulwark."

The prefix *T* (another form of Iphteal) builds abstracts, as ⟦cuneiform⟧ *as-me-a-tu* "a hearing," *te-ni-se-tu* "mankind," *tu-ku-ma-tu* or *tuk-ma-tu* "oppo-ition." Also adjectives as *Tas-me-tu* "she who hears" (the wife of Nebo).

Roots may be increased by prefixing a vowel, as ⟦cuneiform⟧ *al-ca-cat* or *il-ca-cat* " stories," *e-da-khu* " warrior," *im-mi-ru* " youngling," *u-ta-a-ma* " lawgiver."

A word might be lengthened by affixing *ānu* (also *īnu* or *innu* and *ūnu*) to the construct ; 𒈗 𒌋 𒁹 𒑊 *cir-ba-a-nu* " an offering," 𒈾 𒈗 𒁹 𒑊 *sil-dha-a-nu* "a king," 𒀭 𒈗 𒀸 𒑊 *te-er-din-nu* " a descent," 𒁹 𒀀 𒑊 *a-gu-nu* " a crown." Words so formed were collectives.

Gentile nouns were formed by the termination *ai* (fem. *aitu*), as 𒀸 𒈗 𒈗 𒁹 𒁹 *ti-(h)am-ta-ai* " a sailor," 𒈗 𒌋 𒀸 𒈗 𒁹 𒁹 *Ba-bi-la-ai* "a Babylonian," *Dur-Sar-ci-na-ai-ti* " she of Dur-Sargon."

Quadriliterals are occasionally found, as well as quinqueliterals, as *a-sa-ri-du* " first-born," *khar-pa-su* " vehemence," *kha-mi-luhk-khi* " stores," *kha-ba-tsi-il-la-tu* " a lily."

Many Assyrian words are borrowed from Accadian.

PHONOLOGY.

The chief phonetic rules to be remembered are the following :—

1. A sibilant before a dental generally becomes *l*, as *kha-mil-tu* " five " for *kha-mis-tu*.

2. A dental followed by *s* is (together with the sibilant) resolved into *ss* or *s*, as 𒀀 𒈗 𒈗 *ka-as-su* or 𒀀 𒈗 *ka-su* for *kat-su* " his hand."

3. A dental preceded by a sibilant is assimilated to the latter, and when the sibilant is *s* the last rule takes effect, as *its-tsa-bat* for *its-ta-bat* " he is taken," *is-sa-can* and *i-sa-can* for *is-ta-can* " he dwells."

4. After a guttural, the *t* of the secondary conjugations may change to *d* or *dh*, as *ik-dha-rib* for *ik-ta-rib* " he approached."

5. *Kh* in the other Semitic idioms, is frequently replaced in Assyrian by *h*, or lost altogether.

6. Instead of *k* the Babylonian dialect often has *g*, as *ga-tu* for *ka-tu* " hand ;" and this change of letter sometimes makes its way into the Assyrian dialect.

7. *C* frequently takes the place of *k* (especially at the beginning of a word), and also (but more rarely) of *g*, as 〈𒂍 ⊢𒁹𒁹𒁹 𒀹⊱ *ci-ri-bu* for 𒅅𒐊 ⊢𒁹𒁹𒁹 𒀹⊱ *ki-ri-bu* " neighbourhood," 〈𒂍 ⊨𒁹𒁹𒁹 *ci-bit* for 𒅅𒐊 ⊨𒁹𒁹𒁹𒁹 *ki-bit* " command ;" and where the other Semitic dialects prefer the softer consonants (*g*, *z*), Assyrian often combines *c* and *ts* in a root.

8. *N* is generally assimilated to the following consonant, as *id-din* for *in-din* " he gave." Conversely, a double dental may be resolved into *nd* or *nt*.

9. *M* may become *n* before a dental, sibilant, or guttural, as *khan-sa* for *kham-sa* "five," and then be assimilated to the following consonant, as 𒀸⊢𒁹𒁹𒁹 𒀸⊨ *ikhkhar* for *imkhar* "it is present." Conversely, double *b* or double *p* may be resolved into *mb* or *mp*, as *i-nam-bu'* for *i-nab-bu'* " he proclaims."

10. *E* (⊨𒁹𒁹) is always a vowel, and is very frequently used as interchangeable with *i*.

N.B.—The Assyrians had considerable difficulty in adapting the characters of a foreign (Accadian) syllabary to express the sounds of their own language. Hence in the 3rd pers. sing. of a verb, whenever the form requires a prefixed *u* (in Pael, &c.), we have to supply a *y;* thus 𒀀𒁹 must be read *yus*, not *us*, ⊢𒁹𒁹𒁹⊨ *yu*, not *u*. Before 𒁹𒁹, *h* has often to be understood, and sometimes has to be supplied (though not written) after a vowel. *M* and *v* were interchangeable in Accadian, and possibly also in Assyrian ; at all events they are interchangeable in the writing, and ⊨𒁹, e.g., must sometimes be read *ma* and sometimes *va*, 𒀹𒀸 sometimes *am* and sometimes *av*. The chief drawback occasioned by the syllabary was that a final guttural may be read *g*, *c*, or *k*, a final dental *d*, *dh*, or *t*, a final labial *b* or *p*, a final sibilant *s* or *ś*, and even *z* or *ts*. Thus 𒀹𒀸 may be either *tig*, *tic*, or *tik*. Again, 𒁹𒁹 represented both *za* and *tsa*, ⊨𒐊𒐊 *da* or *dha*, 〈𒑱𒀹 *di* or *dhi*, and 𒀹⊱ *bu* or *pu*. Only a certain number of characters contained the vowel *e*. There was no *sh* or *th*.

READING LESSONS.

Extract from the Annals of Tiglath-Pileser I (W.A.I. XVI, col. 8, line 39) :—

(39.) 〔cuneiform〕
li - ta - at   kur   di - ya   ir - nin - tu
The records   of my warriors,   the battle-shout

(40.) 〔cuneiform〕
tam - kha - ri - ya
of my fighting,

〔cuneiform〕
suc - nu - us   naciri
the submission of enemies

(41.) 〔cuneiform〕
tsa - ê - ru - ut   D.P. A - sur   sa   D.P. A - nu   va
hostile   to   Asshur,   whom   Anu   and

〔cuneiform〕
D.P. Rammânu
Rimmon

(42.) 〔cuneiform〕
a - na   si - tsu - ti   is - ru - cu - u - ni
to   destruction   have   given,

(43.) 〔cuneiform〕
i - na   D.P. na - ra a - ya   va   tim - me - ni - ya
on   my tablet   and   my foundation-stone

(44.) 〔cuneiform〕
al dhu - ur
I wrote;

〔cuneiform〕
i - na   bit   D.P. A - nuv   va   D.P. Rammânu
in   the   temple   of Anu   and   Rimmon,

(45.) 〔cuneiform〕
ili   rabi
the gods   great,

〔cuneiform〕
beli - ya
my lords,

(46.) 〔cuneiform〕
a - na   tsa - at   yumi   as - cu - un
for   future   days   I established;

(47.) 〔cuneiform〕
va
and

〔cuneiform〕
D.P. na - ra - a - T   sa D.P. Sam - si D.P. Rammânu
the tablets   of   Samas-Rimmon

(48.) 〔cuneiform〕
a - bi - ya   a - ni - mis
my father   duly

〔cuneiform〕
ab - su - us   D.P. niki
I cleaned :   victims

(49.) 〔cuneiform〕
ak - ki a - na   as - ri - su - nu   u - tir
I sacrificed :   to   their places   I restored (them)

(50.) a-na ar-cat yumi a-na YU-um tsa-a-te (51.) a-na
for future days, for a day long hereafter, for

ma-te-ma ruba ARC-u (52.) e-nu-ma bit D.P. A-nuv va
whatsoever prince hereafter (reigns). When the temple of Anu and

D.P. Rammânu ili (53.) RABU-te beli-ya va śi-gur-ra-a-tu
Rimmon, the gods great, my lords, and the towers

54.) sa-ti-na yu-sal-ba-ru-va (55.) e-na-khu an-khu-śu-nu
these grow old, and decay, their ruins

lu-ud-dis (56.) D.P. na-ra-a-TI-ya va tim-me-ni-ya (57.) ni-mes
may he renew, my tablets and my foundation-stones duly

li-ib-su-us D.P. niki lik-ki (58.) a-na as-ri-su-nu
may he cleanse, victims may he slay, to their places

lu-u-tir (59.) va sum-su it-ti-ya lil-dhu-ur
may he restore, and his name with mine may he write.

(60.) ci-ma ya-ti-ma D.P. A-nuv va D.P. Rammânu (61.) ili rabi
Like myself, may Anu and Rimmon, the great gods,

i-na dhu-ub lib-bi (62.) va ca-sad ir-nin-te dha-bis
in soundness of heart and conquest in battle bountifully

lidh-dhar-ru-su (63.) sa D.P. na-ra-a-TI-ya va tim-me-ni-ya
keep him. He who my inscriptions and my foundation-stones

(64.) 𒀭𒁹𒀭𒁹𒀭 𒀭𒁹𒀭𒁹
i - khab - bu - u   i - śa - pa - nu
shall conceal,   *shall hide,*

(65.) 𒀭𒁹𒀭𒁹𒀭𒁹𒀭𒁹𒀭𒁹
a - na   me   i - na - du - u
to   the   water   shall   lay,

(66.) 𒀭𒁹𒀭𒁹𒀭𒁹𒀭𒁹𒀭𒁹𒀭𒁹
i - na   isati   i - kal - lu - u
with   fire   shall   burn,

(67.) 𒀭𒁹𒀭𒁹𒀭𒁹
i - na   epiri
in   dust

𒀭𒁹𒀭𒁹𒀭𒁹𒀭𒁹𒀭𒁹𒀭𒁹𒀭𒁹
i - ca - ta - mu   i - na   bit   cummi (?)
shall   cover,   *in   a   house   underground (?)*

(68.) 𒀭𒁹𒀭𒁹𒀭𒁹𒀭𒁹𒀭𒁹
a - sar   la - a - ma - ri
a   place   not   seen

𒀭𒁹𒀭𒁹𒀭𒁹𒀭𒁹𒀭𒁹𒀭𒁹
pi - si - ris   i - na - ci - mu
for   interpretation   shall   set,

(69.) 𒀭𒁹𒀭𒁹𒀭𒁹𒀭𒁹𒀭𒁹𒀭𒁹
sum śadh - ra   i - pa - si - dhu - va
the   name   written   shall   erase,   and

(70.) 𒀭𒁹𒀭𒁹𒀭𒁹𒀭𒁹𒀭𒁹𒀭𒁹
sum - su   i - sa - dha - ru   va   mi - lim - ma
his own name   shall   write;   and   an   attack

(71.) 𒀭𒁹𒀭𒁹
lim - na
evil

𒀭𒁹𒀭𒁹𒀭𒁹𒀭𒁹
i - kha - śa - śa - va
shall   devise,   and

(72.) 𒀭𒁹𒀭𒁹𒀭𒁹𒀭𒁹𒀭𒁹𒀭𒁹
a - na   pa - an   D.P.   na - ra - a - TI - ya
against   the   face   of   my   inscriptions

(73.) 𒀭𒁹𒀭𒁹𒀭𒁹
yu - sap - ra - cu
shall   cause   to   break,

(74.) 𒀭𒁹𒀭𒁹𒀭𒁹𒀭𒁹𒀭𒁹
D.P. A - nu   va   D.P. Assuru   ili   rabi
may Anu   and   Assur,   the   gods   great,

𒀭𒁹𒀭𒁹𒀭𒁹
beli - ya
my lords,

(75.) 𒀭𒁹𒀭𒁹𒀭𒁹𒀭𒁹𒀭𒁹𒀭𒁹𒀭𒁹
iz - zi - is   li -   cal - mu - su - va
strongly   injure   him,   and

(76.) 𒀭𒁹𒀭𒁹𒀭𒁹𒀭𒁹𒀭𒁹𒀭𒁹𒀭𒁹𒀭𒁹
ar - ra - ta   ma - ru - us -, ta   li - ru - ru - su
(with) a   curse   grievous   may they curse him;

(77) 𒀭𒁹𒀭𒁹
śarru - śu
his kingdom

𒀭𒁹𒀭𒁹
lis - ci - bu
may they dissipate,

(78.) 𒀭𒁹𒀭𒁹𒀭𒁹𒀭𒁹𒀭𒁹𒀭𒁹
sul   cuśśi   śar(u) - ti - su   li - śu - khu
the ascent of the throne of his kingdom   may they remove

79.) 𒀀𒀀𒀀   𒀀𒀀𒀀   𒀀𒀀   [𒀀]   𒀀𒀀   𒀀
tsab - hi   bilu - ti - su   lu - bal - lu
the armies   of his lordship   may they devour,

(80.) 𒀀𒀀𒀀𒀀
cacci - su
his weapons

𒀀𒀀𒀀𒀀𒀀
lu - sab - bi - ru
may they break,

(81.) 𒀀𒀀𒀀𒀀𒀀𒀀𒀀𒀀𒀀𒀀
a - bi - ic - ti   um - ma - ni - su   lis - cu - nu
the destruction   of his army   may they cause;

82.) 𒀀𒀀𒀀𒀀𒀀𒀀𒀀
i - na   pa - an   naciri - su   ca - mis
in the   presence   of his enemies   wholly

(83.) 𒀀𒀀𒀀𒀀𒀀
lu - se - si - bu - su
may they cause him to dwell;

𒀀𒀀𒀀𒀀𒀀𒀀
D.P. Rammânu i - na   śimmi
may the Air-god with   pestilence

(84.) 𒀀𒀀𒀀𒀀𒀀𒀀𒀀
khul - te mat - śu   li - ib - tsu
destructive his land   cut off;

85.) 𒀀𒀀𒀀𒀀𒀀𒀀𒀀
śu - un - ka   pu - pu - ta   khu - sakh - khu
want   of crops,   famine,   (and)

(86.) 𒀀𒀀𒀀𒀀
pagri   a - na
corpses   against

𒀀𒀀𒀀𒀀
mat - ti - su   lid - di'
his land   may he lay;

(87.) 𒀀𒀀𒀀𒀀𒀀𒀀𒀀𒀀𒀀
ana bil - ut   ma - la - a - ti - su   lik - bi'
against the sovereignty of his full-power   may he speak:

88.) 𒀀𒀀𒀀𒀀𒀀𒀀𒀀𒀀
sum - su   zir - su   ina mati   lu - khal - li - ik
his name,   his seed   in the land   may he destroy.

ANALYSIS.

39. *lītat*, pl. fem., construct form.
    kurdi, for *kurădi*, pl. of *kuradu* "warrior;" perhaps Ar. قدير.
    ya, poss. pron., first person suffix.
    irnintu, with vowel prefix, from רנן "to shout for joy."

40. *tamkhari*, gen. sing., Tiphel derivative from מחר "to be present," facing;"
        hence "opposition" or "fighting."
    sucnus, sing. construct, Shaphel passive deriv. from כנש "to subject."
    náciri, masc. pl. gen., Kal participle of נכר, the Kal of which is not used in
        Hebrew.

41. *tsa'erut*, masc. pl., construct of the Kal part., *tsa'iru* "enemy," Heb. צר.
        The plural is also found under the forms *tsa'eri*, *tsa'iri*, *tsahri* and
        tsayâri. *E* is incorrectly written for *'i*, which stands for *vi*.
    Anu was originally the sky, *Rimmon* was the air-god.

42. *sitsuti*, sing. gen. fem. verbal noun.   Aram. שצא, Targ. שצו "to destroy."
    isrucūni, third pl. masc. perf., Kal of *saracu*.

43. *narā* (preceded by D.P. of "stone" *abnu*), apparently borrowed from
        Accadian. *Narā* (or *narū*) is fem., with pl. *narāti*.
    timmeni, pl. masc., borrowed from Accadian.

44. *aldhur* for *asdhur*, 1st pers. sing. aor. Kal of שטר "to write."
    bīt (for *bayit*), sing. construct; Heb. בית.

45. *ili*, pl. masc. of *'ilu;* Heb. אל.
    rabi, also *rabuti*, masc. pl., adj.; Heb. רב.
    bili or *beli*, pl. masc. of *belu*, Heb. בעל.

46. *tsāt*, fem. pl. construct; abstract noun from יצא (Ass. *atsu*) "to go forth"
        (literally "the goings forth," "that which will go forth").
    yumi, pl. masc. of *yumu*, Heb. יום.
    ascun, 1st pers. sing. aor. Kal of שכן (originally Shaphel of כון).

48. *'abi*, gen. sing. masc. of *abu* (אב).

'animes, adverb in *-is* formed from pl. of *'anu*, "suitably, fitly." Cp. Ar. انى

absus, 1st per. sing. aor. Kal of בשש "to cleanse."

niki, pl. of *niku* "offering," "sacrifice;" Heb. נקה.

49. *akki*, 1st pers. sing. aor. Kal of נקה (*naku'u*), from which *niku* is derived.

'asri, pl. of *'asru*, "a place;" Aram. (& Ar.) אתר.

utir, 1st pers. sing. aor. Aphel of *tāru*, "to come back," become," "be;" Heb. תור "to go about."

50. *'arcāt*, pl. fem. construct of an abstract *'arcu* for *aricu*, "after" p. ארך.

yum tsāte literally "day of the future;" *yum* in construct sing., *tsāte* abstract fem. pl.

51. *matema* "at any time," "at any place;" Cp. Heb. מתי "when."

rubu, from רב, literally "a great one."

52. *enuma*, adverb compounded of *enu* (Ar. عدى عنا), and the pron. *ma* "that."

53. *sigurrātu*, pl. fem. of *sigurrǎtu*, "a closed place," hence "a temple-tower" or observatory, from סגר. It is written *ziggurrǎtu* in the Babylonian dialect.

54. *sātina*, pl. fem. of the pron. *su'atu*, *sātu*, agreeing with *sigurrātu*.

yusalbaru-va, 3rd pers. masc. aor. Shaphel of *labaru* "to be old," with the enclitic conjunction *va* (ו) "and."

55. *enakhu*, 3rd. pers. masc. pl. aor. Kal of ענח.

'ankhusunu, for *ankhut-sunu*, *t* + *s* being replaced not only by *t* + *s*, but also by *s* alone.

ankhut is pl. masc. from *'ankhu* a subst. derived from ענח, *'ayin* becoming *'a*.

luddis, 3rd sing. masc. Precative Aphel of *hadasu* "to be new." Cp. Heb. חדש.

57. *nimes* for *'animes*, as in line 48. Verbs פ"א drop their initial radical in many forms. (See my *Assyrian Grammar*, p. 108).

libsus, 3rd masc. sing. prec. Kal from *basasu* (as above).

likki', 3rd masc. sing. prec. Kal from *niku'u* (as above), the nasal being assimilated to the following letter.

58. *lutir*, 3rd masc. sing. prec. Aphel of *tāru* (as above).

59.   *sum*, sing. masc. construct of *sumu* "a name;" Heb. שם.

      itti, preposition; Heb. את.

      lildhur, 3rd masc. sing. prec. Kal of *sadharu* (as above).

60.   *yatima*, 1st pers. pron., compounded of *ya* "I," the suffix *ti*, and the pron. *ma*.

61.   *dhub*, sing. construct of the subst. *dhubu;* Heb. טוב (see line 62).

      libbi, gen. sing. of *libbu* "heart;" Heb לב.

62.   *casad*, sing. masc. construct of *casadu* "a possession," from *casadu* "to conquer."

      irninte, gen. sing. of the collective *irnintu* (as above); "possession of the battle-cry " = " victory in battle."

      dhābis, adverb in *-is* from *dhabu* "good" (as in line 61). *Dhābu* is for *dhăvăbu*.

      lidhdharru, 3rd pl. masc. prec. Kal of *nadharu* "to guard;" Heb. נטר.

64.   *ikhabbu'u*, 3rd sing. masc. future Kal of *khabū* "to hide;" Heb. חבא. (For the form see my *Assyrian Grammar*, pp. 52, 53, 69).

      isápanu for *isappanu*, 3rd sing. masc. fut. Kal of *sapanu* "to sweep away," with *a* for *i* in the 3rd syllable; Cp. Heb. ספה.

65.   *me*, pl. masc. of *mu* "a drop of water." The reduplicated pl. *mami* also occurs; Heb. מים.

      inádu'u for *inaddu'u*, 3rd sing. masc. fut. Kal of *nadu'u* "to place;" Cp. Ar. نَ.

66.   *'isati*, pl. gen. fem. of *'isu* "fire" (Heb. אש).

      ikallu'u, 3rd sing. masc. fut. Kal of קלה "to burn" (as in Heb. and Ar.)

67.   *epiri*, pl. of *ipru* or *epru* "dust;" Heb. עפר.

      icátumu for *icattumu*, 3rd sing. masc. fut. Kal of כתם, with *u* instead of *i* in the 3rd syllable.

      bit cummi (?). Conjectural transliteration. The first ideograph is "house" (*bitu*), the second "high" or "precious" (*ellu*), and the third "god" (*'ilu*). The second and third, however, must be taken together as a compound ideograph, and perhaps denote the Assyrian Plutus.

68. *lâ amari; lâ* "not" (Heb. לא), *amari*, the gen. masc. pl. after construct *asar* of the adjective *amaru* "seen;" therefore literally "things seen" (Cp. Heb. אור).

pisiris, adverb, in -*is* from *pisiru* "an interpretation" (Heb. and Aram. פשר).

inácimu for *inaccimu*, 3rd sing. masc. fut. Kal of נכם "to take."

69. *ipásidhu* for *ipassidhu*, 3rd sing. masc. fut. Kal of *pasadhu* "to strip" (Heb. פשט).

70. *isadharu* for *isadhdharu* (with *a* for *i*), 3rd sing. masc. fut. Kal of *sadharu* (as above).

milimma, acc. sing. of *milimma* or *milimmu*, from לוה "to cleave to." A variant reading gives *lumima* or *luviva*, apparently from the same root.

71. *limna*, acc. sing. masc. of the adj. *limnu* (for *limunu*), agreeing with *milimma;* perhaps akin to Heb. (and Ar.) לחם "to fight."

ikhasasa-va for *ikhassasa*, 3rd sing. masc. fut. Kal of *khasasu*, with final *u* changed to -*a* through the influence of the same vowel in both the following and the preceding syllables; Cp. Æth., *khasasa* "to investigate;" Ar. *khassa.*

72. *pān*, construct of *pānu* "face;" Heb. פנים.

73. *yusapracu*, 3rd sing. masc. fut. Shaphel of פרך "to break."

75. *'izzis*, adverb in -*is*, from *'izzu* "strong;" Heb. עז.

licálmu, 3rd pl. masc. prec. Pael of כלם "to injure" or "revile," contracted from *licallĭmu.*

76. *'arrăti*, sing. fem. subst., from ארר "to curse" (see *liruru* below).

marusta for *marutsta*, fem. adj., agreeing with *'arrati*, from מרץ "to be violent" or "hard."

liruru, 3rd pl. masc. prec. Kal of ארר.

77. *sarrusu* for *sarrut-su; sarrut* fem. abstract sing. construct. Heb. שר "king."

liscibu, 3rd pl. masc. prec. Kal of *sacabu* "to pour out;" Ar. سكب

9*

78. *sul*, construct sing. of *sūlu* "ascent;" Shaphel pass. derivative of עלה "to ascend." The ideograph may also be read *isid* "foundation" (Heb. יסוד).

  eussu, construct sing. of *cussu'u* "throne" (as in Heb.)

  lišukhu for *lissukhu*, 3rd pl. masc. prec. Kal of כסח "to remove."

79. *tsabhi*, pl. construct of *tsabu* (Heb. צבא) "an army."

  luballu, 3rd pl. masc. prec. Pael of בלע "to devour."

80. *cacci*, pl. of *caccu* "a weapon;" perhaps for *carci* (Aram. כרך "armour").

  lusabbiru, 3rd pl. masc. prec. Pael of שבר "to break."

81. *'abicti*, fem. abstract; Cp. Heb. הפך "to destroy."

  'ummani, gen. sing. fem. of *'ummanu* "army;" Cp. Heb. המון "multitude."

  liscunu, 3rd pers. masc. pl. prec. Kal of *sacanu* (as above).

82. *camis*, adverb in *-is*, from *camu*; Cp. Ar. كلّ.

83. *lusesibu*, 3rd pers. pl. masc. prec. Shaphel of *asibu* "to dwell;" Heb. ישב.

  simmi, gen. sing. masc. of *simmu* "a plague;" Cp. Heb. שמם.

84. *khulte*, adj. agreeing with *simmi*; Cp. Heb. חלה. The Semitic root seems to have been borrowed from Accadian.

  mat, construct sing. of *madu* or *mātu* "country," of Accadian origin (*ma-da*); Cp. Aram. מתא. (See line 86).

  libtsu, 3rd pl. masc. prec. Kal of בצע "to cut off."

85. *sunka*, acc. sing. of *sunku*; Cp. Talm. סנוק "scantiness," "frugality."

  bubuta, acc. sing. of *bubutu* "crops;" perhaps Heb. ניב "fruit" may be compared. *Bubuta* is in opposition to *sunka*.

  khusakhkha, acc. sing. of *khusakhkhu* "need" (Aram. חסה).

86. *pagri*, acc. pl. masc. of *pagru* "a corpse" (Heb. פגר).

  matti for *madti* (or perhaps *māti*), gen. sing. of *mātu* (see line 84).

  liddi', 3rd pers. sing. masc. prec. Kal of נדה (see above).

87. *malātišu* for *malātit-su*; *malātit*, construct of abstract in ־ית, from *malāti*, pl. fem., from מלא "to fill."

  likbi', 3rd sing. masc. prec. Kal of קבה (in Heb., "to curse").

88. *zir*, construct sing. of *zir'u* or *zer'u* "seed" (Heb. זרע).

  lukhallik, 3rd sing. masc. prec. Pael of חלק ("to divide," hence) "to scatter," "destroy."

THE LEGEND OF ISTAR.—OBVERSE.

The Cuneiform Characters to be supplied by the Student.

A-na   mat   NU-GA-A   kak-ka-ri   i-di-ya
To the land of Hades,   regions of corruption,

D.P.   Istaru   banat   D.P.   Śini   u-zu-un-sa   [ci-nis]
Istar,   daughter of the Moon-god,   her attention   [determinedly]

is - cun - va   banat   D.P.   śini   u - zu - un - [sa   is - cun]
fixed,   and   the daughter of the Moon-god   her attention   fixed

a - na   bit   e - di - e   su - bat   'il Ir - kal - la
(to go) to the house of corruption,   the dwelling   of the deity Irkalla;

a - na   biti   sa   e - ri - bu - su   la   a - tsu - u
to   the house whose   entrance (is)   without exit,

a - na   khar - ra - ni   sa   a - lac - ta - su   la ta - ai - rat (u)
to   the road   whose   way (is)   without return,

a - na   biti   sa   e - ri - bu - su   zu - um - mu - u   mu - u - ra
to   the house (at) whose   entrance   they bridle in   the light;

a - sar   epru mahdu   bu - bu - uś - śu - nu   a - cal - su - nu   dhi - idh - dhu
a place (where)   dust   much   (is) their food,   their victuals   (is) mud;

nu - u - ru   ul   im - ma - ru   ina   e - dhu - ti   as - bā
(where) light not   they see,   in   darkness   they dwell; and

cal (?) - su - ma   cima   its - tsu - ri   tsu - bat cap-pi
?   like   birds (is)   the erecting of (their) wings;

eli   dalti   u   sac - cul - sa   mukh   ep - ru
over   the door   and   its wainscoting   abundance   of dust.

D.P. Istaru   a - na   bâbi   D.P.   NU-GA-A   ina   ca - sa - di - sa
Istar,   to (at) the gate   of Hades   at   her arrival

a - na   ni - gab   ba - a - bi   a - ma - tuv   iz - zac - car
to   the porter   of the gate   (his) duty   reminds;

a - na   ni - gab   me - e   pi - ta̤   ba - ab - ca
to   the porter   of the waters: Open   thy gate!

15. pi - ta - a   ba - ab - ca - va   lu   ir - ru - ba   a - na - cu
     Open   thy gate,   and let   me enter in;

16. sum - ma   la   ta - pat - ta - a   ba - a - bu   la   ir - ru - ba   a - na - cu
     if   not   thou openest   the gate (and) not   I enter in,

17. a - makh - kha - ats   dal - tuv   śic - cu - ru   a - sab - bir
     I force   the gate,   the bolt   I break,

18. a - makh - kha - ats   śi - ip - pu   va   u - sa - pal - cit   dalâti
     I force   the threshold,   and   I cross   the doors,

19. u - se - el - la   mi - tu - ti   acili   pal - dhu - ti
     I raise   the dead,   the devourers   of the living;

20. eli   pal - dhu - ti   i - ma - hi - du   mi - tu - ti
     above the   living   exceed   the dead.

ANALYSIS.

1. The Accadian MAD NU-GA-A is literally "land of the not returning,"
    ga'a being the participle of *gā* "to return" (see *Syllabary*). It is
    rendered in Ass. by *mat-la-naciri*. "The land from whence is no
    return" is a good name for Hades.
    kakkari, acc. pl. of *kakkaru*, Heb. כבר (see my *Assyrian Grammar*, p. 29).
    édi, written *éde* in line 4, gen. sing. of *édu* "corruption," as Dr. Schrader has
    well explained it from עדה "to pass away."

2. *Istar*, the Hebrew Ashtoreth (Astarte), the Moon-goddess and Semitic
    Venus.
    bánat, construct sing. fem. of *banatu* (also *bintu*, i.e. *binitu*) "daughter"
    (Heb. בת). Sin, the Moon-god.
    'uzun, construct sing. of *'uzunu* or *'uznu* "ear" (Heb. אזן).
    cinis ?, supplied by Dr. Schrader, adverb in *-is* from adj. *cinu* (כן).

3. *iscun*, 3rd sing. masc. aor. of *sacanu*. It will be noticed that here as
    frequently elsewhere a feminine nominative is joined to a masc. verb.

4. *subat*, construct sing. fem. of *subătu* from ישב "to sit" or "dwell."

5. *eribu*, nom. sing. masc. infinitive (or verbal noun) from ערב "to enter" or "descend."

   'atsu, nom. sing. masc. verbal noun from יצא "to go out." The literal translation of the line is "of which its entering (there is) no outgoing."

6. *khar-ra-ni*, sing. oblique case of *kharranu*, a word originally borrowed from Accadian, which gave a name to the city of Kharran or Haran (Gen. xi. 31, &c.)

   'alacta or *halacta*, sing. fem. of *halactu* from הלך "to go."

   tairat for *tairatu* (as often in the case of characters which denote syllables beginning and ending with a consonant), for *tayartu*, sing. fem. from תור "to return."

7. *zummu*, 3rd pl. masc. (used impersonally) Permansive (or Perfect) Palel of זום. Cp. Targ. זמם "bridle." In Ass. *zumani* "impassable" is used of roads.

   nura, acc. sing. of *nuru* "light" (so in Heb. [נר], Aram. and Ar.)

8. *'asar* "a place" (*see above*) often has the relative *sa* ("in which," "where") understood after it.

   mahdu, nom. sing. masc. adj. agreeing with *epru*. Cp. Heb. מאד.

   bubussunu for *bubut-sunu* (*see above*).

   'acal, construct sing. of the verbal noun *acalu* "food," from אכל "to eat."

   dhidhdhu, nom. sing. in opposition to *acal*. Heb. טיט.

9. *immaru*, 3rd pers. pl. masc. present Kal of נמר, contracted from *inammaru*.

   edhuti, gen. sing. of *edhutu* "darkness," from עטה, "to hide," as Dr. Schrader has pointed out.

   'asbā, contracted from *asbū-a* for *asbū-va*, 3rd pl. masc. Permansive (or Perfect) Kal of *'asabu*, contracted from *'asibu* (also *yasibu*), with the enclitic conjunction.

10. The first word I cannot read.

    'itstsuri, pl. masc. of *'itstsuru* "a bird" (Ar. عصفور, Heb. צפור).

    tsubat, construct sing. fem. of *tsubātu* "a placing," from יצב. The reading and meaning of the word, however, are uncertain.

    cappi, pl. masc. of *cappu*, contracted from *canapu* (Heb. כנף), the double letter resulting from the assimilation of the nasal.

11. *dalti*, gen. sing. fem. of *daltu* (for *dalătu*) "door." (So in Heb.)

   saccul, construct sing. of *sacculu*, which Dr. Schrader has well compared with Ar. شكل "likeness." A Syllabary makes *mescalū* a synonyme of *daltu*.

   mukh, construct sing. of *mukhkhu*, from the adjective *makh*, which was borrowed from Accadian.

12. *bâbi*, gen. sing. of *bâbu* "gate" (as in Heb., &c.)

   casidi, gen. sing. masc. of the verbal noun *casadu* "a reaching," from *casadu* "to take;" Cp. Ar. كشد.

13. *nigab*, construct sing. masc. Dr. Schrader derives it from a root נקף "to go round."

   'amātuv, sing. fem. for *'amantuv* "fealty," "duty;" Heb. אמת "faithfulness."

   izzaccar, for *iztaccar*, 3rd sing. masc. present Iphteal of זכר.

14. *mē* "waters" (as above).

   pitā, for *piti-a* with the augment of motion, 2nd sing. masc. imperative Kal of *patâ* "to open;" Heb. פתח. See also next line.

15. *irruba*, 1st pers. sing. masc. aor. Kal with augment of motion, from *eribu*. The *ayin* of the first syllable is replaced by a reduplication of the 2nd radical.

16. *summa*, adverb, perhaps from שום "to place."

   tapattā, 2nd pers. sing. present Kal with augment of motion, from *patā*.

17. *amakhkhats*, 1st pers. sing. pres. Kal of מחץ.

   siccuru, sing. noun (a pael derivative); Cp. Aram. סכרא "bolt."

   asabbir, 1st pers. sing. pres. Kal of שבר.

18. *sippu*, sing. noun; Heb. סף.

   usapalcit, 1st pers. sing. aor. Shaphel of the quadriliteral *palcitu*; Cp. Ar. فلق (?)

19. *usella*, 1st pers. sing. pres. Shaphel of עלה "to ascend," with *ll* on account of the *ayin*.

   mitūti, pl. masc. part. pass. Kal of מות "to die."

   acili, pl. construct part. pres. Kal of *acalu*, "to eat."

   paldhūti, pl. masc. part. Kal of *paladhu* or *baladhu*, "to live;" Cp. Heb. פלט.

20. *imahidu*, 3rd pers. pl. masc. pres. Kal of *mahadu* (whence *mahdu*, "much," line 7).

THE SACRIFICE OF CHILDREN (K 5139).

The transliteration to be supplied by the Student.

1. 𒀭 ... ...
    ?   *may   he   remove,   and*

2. ... ...
  the   offspring   who   raises   the   head   among   men,

3. ... ...
  the   offspring   for   his   life   he   gave,

4. ... ...
  the head   of   the   offspring   for   the   head   of   the   man   he   gave,

5. ... ...
  the brow   of   the   offspring   for   the   brow   of   the   man   he   gave,

6. ... ...
  the breast   of   the   offspring   for   the   breast   of   the   man   he   gave.

NOTES.

1. From נסׄח.

2. Cp. Ar. ورص "to bear eggs." Notice the correct use of the case-endings in this inscription.

    The Accadian SAK ILA (so *gadhu-la* is to be read), literally "head-raising," must be replaced by some corresponding Ass. adj. or part. of which -*u* is the phonetic complement. The Syllabaries render the words by *risa-nasū*.

    aveluti, abstract fem. sing.

5. *cisad* (see *casadi* above).

FROM THE HYMN TO SIN (K. 2861).

The English translation to be supplied by the Student.

1. bil - luv   e - bil - li   ili   sa   ina   same   u   irtsi - tiv
   e - dis - si -su   tsi - i - ru

2. a - bu   D.P. Na - an - nar   bel - luv   'ilu   dhabu   e - bil - li   ili

3. a - bu   D.P. Na - an - nar   bil - luv   i - lu   rab-u   e - bil- li   ili

4. a - bu   D.P. Na - an - nar   bil- luv   D.P. Śinu   e - bil - li   ili

5. a - bu   D.P. Na - an - nar   be - el   U - ri - e   e - bil - li   ili

6. a - bu   D.P. Na - an - nar   be - el   bit   śamulli   e - bil- li   ili

7. a - bu   D.P.   Na - an - nar   be - el   a - gi - e   su - bu - u
   e - bil   li   ili

8. a - bu   D.P. Na - an - nar   sa   śar - ru - tav   ra - bis   suc - lu - luv
   e - bil- li   ili

9. a - bu   D.P.   Na - an - nar   sa   ina   ti - di - ic   ru - bu - tav
   i - nad - di -khu   e - bil- li   ili

0. [cuneiform signs]

bú - ru   ik - du   sa   kar - ni   gab - ba - ru   sa   mes - ri - ti

[cuneiform signs]

suc - lu - luv   sic - ni   uc - ni - i   sac - nu

1. [cuneiform signs]

cu - uz - bu - u   la - la - a   ma - lu - u

NOTES.

1. *ebilli*, 3rd pers. masc. aor. (with *i* termination) "he rules," from עבל another
form of בעל.

   'edissi-su "he alone," anomalously formed from adverb *édis*.

   tsīru, "supreme."

2. *Nannar*, "the luminary," a name of Sin, the Moon-god.

5. *Ure*, gen. of Ur, the city of Uru (now *Mugheir*).

5. *samulli* (in Accadian SIR-GAL) = "image." Heb. סמל.

7. *age* = "of crowns"; (the Semitic root was borrowed from Accadian).

   subū, Shaphel pass. part. of בוא "to come" (referring to the moon's motion).

8. *suclulu*, Shaphalel pass. part. of יכל "to be able," "to prevail."

9. *tidic*, construct sing. of a (Tiphel) noun with prefixed *t*, from *dācu* (= Heb.
רכה).

   inaddikhu = "he will drive."

0. *bu'-ru*, or *buhru* = "brilliance" (as in Ar.)

   ikdu = "mighty" (of Accadian origin).

   mesriti = "the feet" or "limbs." Dr. Schrader compares the Heb. שרין
"coat of mail," which in Aram. signifies "the artery" or "nerve."

   sicni = "habitations."

   ucnī = "marble" (probably of Accadian origin).

1. *cuzbū* = "beauty." Norris compares Heb. קצב.

   lalā = "fulness," from Accadian *lal*, "to fill" (see *Syllabary*).

Hunting Inscriptions of Assur-bani-pal (W.A.I. I, pl. 7).

The text to be transliterated by the Student.

1. 𒀭 ⸝ ⸝ . ⸝ ⸝ . ⸝ . ⸝ . ⸝ . ⸝ . ⸝ .
   ⸝ ⸝ ⸝ . ⸝ ⸝ ⸝ . ⸝ ⸝ ⸝ ⸝ .

2. ⸝ ⸝ ⸝ ⸝ ⸝ . ⸝ ⸝ ⸝ . ⸝ . ⸝ ⸝ ⸝ .
   ⸝ ⸝ ⸝ ⸝ . ⸝ ⸝ ⸝ . ⸝ . ⸝ ⸝ . ⸝ . ⸝ . ⸝ .

3. ⸝ ⸝ . ⸝ ⸝ . ⸝ ⸝ ⸝ . ⸝ ⸝ ⸝ . ⸝ ⸝ . ⸝ ⸝ .
   ⸝ ⸝ ⸝ ⸝ . ⸝ ⸝ . ⸝ ⸝ . ⸝ ⸝ ⸝ . ⸝ ⸝ .

NOTES.

1. ⸝⸝⸝ "the good god," became the usual designation of Assur.

   ⸝⸝ ⸝⸝ ⸝⸝⸝ "the lady of the abyss," or "underworld," was a title of Beltis.
   'emuci, pl. of the substantive *'emucu,* "a deep intelligence," "a divinity"
   (Heb. עמק).

2. *yusatlimu's,* "they conferred on him," 3rd pl. masc. aor. Shaphel of *talamu,*
   with the possessive pronoun *s* contracted from *su.*

   ⸝⸝ ⸝⸝⸝ "great dog," was the Accadian name of "the lion" (Ass. *nesu*).
   adducu, Heb. דכה.; notice the tense.

   ⸝ ⸝⸝ ⸝⸝ ⸝ means "an altar," with the D.P. of *wood* and the phonetic
   complement *ānu*; but the reading of the ideograph is uncertain.

   izzitu, adj. ; Cp. Heb. עז.

   ⸝⸝ ⸝⸝ "the goddess 15," symbol of Istar.

3. *azkup,* root זקף.

   mukhkhuru, "an offering," from מהר "to present."

   sun, contracted for *sunu.*

The text to be transliterated by the student.

1. [cuneiform text]

2. [cuneiform text]

3. [cuneiform text]

NOTES.

1. *multahti*, "renown," fem. abstract from the Iphteal part. of שׁאה "to make a noise," with *l* before *t* for *s*.

   issu, "fierce;" Cp. Heb. עסס (Aram. עטי) "to tread," "oppress."

2. *sa* = "of whom."

   tsir, "back" (Ar. ظهر).

   tuculti = "service."

   takhazi, weakened from *takhatsi*, for *takhkhatsi* (*tamkhatsi*) "battle," from מחץ.

3. D.P. *asmare*, "spears;" Cp. Heb. מסמר "a nail."

   aznik = "I pierced" (Cp. Heb. זֵק "a dart," זנק "to shoot forth"). The printed text gives *azkhul*, which must be wrong.

   zumur, "body;" ideograph of "body" or "skin," with phonetic complement *mur*. Delitzsch compares the Talmud צטורה "wind in the stomach."

The text to be transliterated by the Student.

1. 𒀹 [cuneiform signs]

2. [cuneiform signs]
   [cuneiform signs]

3. [cuneiform signs]
   [cuneiform signs]

4. [cuneiform signs]
   [cuneiform signs]

NOTES.

2. *melulti rubuti* "the action" or "right of sovereignty;" *melulti*, fem. abstract from עלל "to act" (especially "to act wonderfully").

3. *cibit* = "command" (with weakened guttural from קבה).

   [cuneiform] = Adar.

   [cuneiform] = Nergal.

   ticli "ministers;" same root as *tucultu*.

4. D.P. *khutbale* = "ropes," Heb. חבל.

   mukhkha = "over" (of Accadian derivation).

   umatti', 1st pers. aor. Pael, "I stretched." Ar. الخ "to stretch a cord."

From the Black Obelisk of SHALMANESER (Layard's Insc. pl. 96 l. 159.)

The text to be transliterated by the Student.

59. [cuneiform text]

60. [cuneiform text]

61. [cuneiform text]

62. [cuneiform text]

63. [cuneiform text]

64. [cuneiform text]

65. [cuneiform text]

66. [cuneiform text]

67. [cuneiform text]

168. 𒂊𒈠𒉌 . 𒐖 𒂊𒐖 . 𒈨 . 𒈾𒂊𒈠𒐖 . 𒈨 𒍝 𒈨 . 𒂊𒈠𒐖 . 𒅅 𒈨𒐖 . 𒐖𒐖𒐖 .
𒈠𒐖 𒂊𒈠𒐖 𒍝𒐖𒐖 . 𒐖 𒈨𒐖 . 𒂊𒐖𒈨 . 𒌋 . 𒐖𒐖 𒈬 𒐖 .
𒍝 𒊩𒈨 𒐖 .

169. 𒂊𒌋𒍝 𒈬 𒂊𒐖 . 𒂊𒐖𒐖 𒂊𒐖 𒅖 𒂊𒐖 𒐖 . 𒂊𒐖 . 𒐖𒐖 𒂊𒌋 . 𒐕 . 𒐖𒐖 𒅅 .
𒂊𒐖𒈨 𒅖 . 𒌋 . 𒂊𒈠𒐖𒐖 𒐖 𒂊𒈠𒐖 . 𒐕 . 𒍝 𒍝𒐖 .

NOTES.

159. "In my 30 campaigns" = "In my 30th campaign."

The city of Calkhi represents the Calah of Scripture.

cī utsbacuni "when I was stopping," 1st pers. sing. Permansive Kal of וצב with conditional suffix *ni.*

Dayan-Assur, "Assur is judge," was the name of the Tartan ("strong chief") or generalissimo.

160. 𒍝 𒈬 𒐖 ("host-many") = "armies."

panat, pl. fem. construct of *pānu.*

umāhir "I urged on" (Heb. מהר).

The Upper Zab is here referred to.

161. *'ebir* "I crossed."

lib = "middle" (the heart being the middle of a thing).

Read *'alāni* from *alu* (Heb. אהל "tent"); the phonetic complement *ni* shows how the plural sign is to be read.

icdarrib, Iphteal of *carabu* "to approach" (Heb. קרב), *t* being changed into *d* after *c.*

mādātu = "tribute," literally "gift;" for *mandattu* (*mandantu*), from *nadanu* (Heb. נתן).

162. *attakhar* "I received;" Iphteal of מחר.

163. *attusir* "I departed;" Ittaphal of וסר, another form of *vassaru* "to leave" (Cp. Heb. מסר).

165. These are the Minni of the Old Testament.

namurrat, fem. sing. construct from *namaru* "to see."

166. *ippar* "he fled;" Cp. Heb. עבר, *p* in Assyrian replacing *b*.

uvaśśir; see line 163.

suzub, Shaphel pass. verbal noun from עזב "to save."

napisti "life;" the plural sign is not to be read in Assyrian.

eli "he went up" from עלה.

167. *artedi*, Iphteal from רדה (Heb. ירד) "to descend."

sāsu "spoil" (Cp. Heb. שסה).

mani = "countable number." (Heb. מנה).

168. *abbal* "I strew down" (Heb. נפל).

āgur for *aggur* "I dug up" (Heb. נקר).

asrup "I burned" (Heb. שרף).

169. *limetu* from לוה "to cleave to."

acsud "I took," with phonetic complement *ud*.

Lightning Source UK Ltd.
Milton Keynes UK
UKHW041139211218
334365UK00002B/201/P